# Student Activity Workbook
## to Accompany
# West's Business and Personal Law

## Sonya Rosenglick
*Florida School of Business, Tampa, FL*

*West Publishing Company*

Minneapolis/St. Paul   New York   Los Angeles   San Francisco

**WEST'S COMMITMENT TO THE ENVIRONMENT**

In 1906, West Publishing Company began recycling materials left over from the production of books. This began a tradition of efficient and responsible use of resources. Today, up to 95% of our legal books and 70% of our college texts and school texts are printed on recycled, acid-free stock. West also recycles nearly 22 million pounds of scrap paper annually—the equivalent of 181,717 trees. Since the 1960s, West has devised ways to capture and recycle waste inks, solvents, oils, and vapors created in the printing process. We also recycle plastics of all kinds, wood, glass, corrugated cardboard, and batteries, and have eliminated the use of Styrofoam book packaging. We at West are proud of the longevity and the scope of our commitment to the environment.

Production, Prepress, Printing and Binding by West Publishing Company.

# Chapter 1
## Introduction to the Law

# Chapter 2
## Law and Individual Rights

# Chapter 3
## Courts and the Legal System

# Chapter 4
## Criminal Law

# Chapter 5
## Tort Law

# Chapter 6
## Ethics and Social Responsibility

# Chapter 7
## Introduction to Contracts

## Chapter 8
## Offer and Acceptance

## Chapter 9
## Consideration and Capacity

## Chapter 10
## Legality and Genuineness of Assent

## Chapter 11
## Writing and Form

## Chapter 12
## Third Party Rights and Discharge

## Chapter 13
## Breach and Remedies

## Chapter 14
## Sales

# CHAPTER 1 - VOCABULARY ACTIVITY

**Directions:** Fill in the blank space with the vocabulary term that best completes each sentence. Then write the term on the appropriate line in the puzzle. Use the letters in the boxed spaces to form the answer for question number 11. *Note: Definitions for the vocabulary terms can be found in the margins of the chapter as well as in the glossary of the student text.*

1. The person who brings an action in court against another person is known as a _____.

2. The compilation of rules and statutes on a certain subject is known as a _____.

3. A _____ defines the powers and limits of a government.

4. It is extremely helpful to understand the _____ if you are dealing with the business world. This code was created to make the law on commercial contracts consistent with common business practices.

5. A law originated by the U.S. Congress or a state legislative body, and passed by that body is known as a _____.

6. The term _____ refers to a written decision of the court. This document details the reason for the decision, the rules of law that apply, and the judgement.

7. The _____ system originally developed under the English court system. It is known as judge-made-law.

8. The person against whom an action in court is brought is known as a _____.

9. Someone who has been legally wronged has a _____; the enforcement of a right or compensation for the violation of a right.

10. People selected to make decisions based on facts presented in a legal action serve on a _____.

## WORD PUZZLE

1. ☐ __ __ __ __ __ __ __ __

2. __ __ __ ☐

3. __ __ __ __ ☐ __ __ __ __ __ __

4. __ __ ☐ __ __ __ __

   __ __ __ __ __ __ __ __ __ __ __ __

5. __ ☐ __ __ __ __ __

6. __ __ ☐ __ __ __ __

7. __ __ __ __ ☐ __

8. __ __ __ __ ☐ __ __ __ __

9. __ __ __ ☐ __ __

10. __ __ ☐ __

11. The _____ is the party who initiates a proceeding in equity.

# CHAPTER 1 - FACTS AND IDEAS

**Directions:** Write short answers for each of the following questions on the lines provided. You can use your book to help you find the answers. *Note: You may want to use this activity to study for the chapter test.*

1. What doctrine applies to common law? How is this doctrine related to common law?

   _____

   _____

   _____

2. Why is constitutional law important?

   _____

   _____

   _____

3. What is the difference between statutory law and administrative law?

   _____

   _____

   _____

4. Does the United States have an adversarial or inquisitorial system of justice? Explain.

   _____

   _____

   _____

5. What is the difference between civil law and criminal law?

   _____

   _____

   _____

6. Are state governments allowed to pass laws and regulations on the same subject matter as the federal government? Why, or why not?

_____

_____

_____

7. Are both procedural law and substantive law necessary for our legal system to function? Explain.

_____

_____

_____

8. Describe the evolution of actions in equity.

_____

_____

_____

9. What is the Uniform Commercial Code? Why is it important?

_____

_____

_____

10. How can you tell the difference between a federal court decision and a state court decision?

_____

_____

_____

# CHAPTER 1 - CRITICAL THINKING ACTIVITY

**Directions:** Throughout the student text, *Legal Focus* features are used to provide examples of important legal concepts. Choose two of the concepts below and write your own *Legal Focus* examples or legal focus problems that help to explain the concepts.

a. **civil law** - Law related to the duties that exist generally between persons or between persons and the government except the duty not to commit crimes.

b. **criminal law** - Law related to wrongs committed against the public, punishable by fines, imprisonment, or both

c. **equity** - A branch of law supplying special rules and procedures when legal rules are inadequate to promote justice and fairness

d. **federal law** - Federal law consists of the U.S. Constitution, statutes originated by Congress, treaties and presidential orders, rules, and regulations created by federal administrative agencies, and decisions of federal courts.

1. **Legal Focus**

_____

_____

_____

_____

_____

_____

_____

## 2. Legal Focus

_____

_____

_____

_____

_____

_____

_____

_____

_____

# CHAPTER 2 - VOCABULARY ACTIVITY

**Directions:** Fill in the blank with the appropriate vocabulary term found in the chapter which best completes the sentence. Use the letters from the numbered space to form a scrambled vocabulary term from the chapter; unscramble the letters to form the vocabulary term from the chapter. Define the term.

1. Laws which protect our individual rights and are the first ten amendments to the Constitution are called the _____.

   ___ ___ ___ ___   ___ ___   ___ ___ ___ ___ ⬜

2. A federal or state law is considered _____ if it violates the U. S. Constitution.

   ___ ___ ⬜ ___ ___   ___ ___   ___ ___ ___ ___ ___

3. The rights of life, liberty, and the pursuit of happiness are based on _____.

   ___ ___ ___ ___ ⬜ ___ ___   ___ ___ ___

4. A national system of government which coexists with various state governments is called _____.

   ___ ⬜ ___ ___ ___ ___ ___ ___ ___ ___

5. The clause which prohibits the government from establishing a state religion is the _____ clause.

   ___ ___ ___ ___ ___ ___ ___ ___ ___ ___ ___ ___ ⬜

6. The _____ powers give power to each state to protect and promote the health, safety, and welfare of its citizens.

   ___ ⬜ ___ ___ ___ ___

7. The clause which prohibits the government from interfering in people's practice of religion is called the _____ clause.

   ___ ___ ___ ___   ___ ___ ___ ___ ___ ⬜ ___ ___

8. The _____ clause allows the federal government the right to regulate most business activities in the United States.

___ ___ ___ ___ ___ ___ ___ ☐

9. The United States _____ is considered the supreme law of the land in the United States.

___ ___ ☐ ___ ___ ___ ___ ___ ___ ___ ___ ___

10. Rights that are considered beyond the power of government or deny are the _____ rights.

___ ___ ___ ___ ___ ☐ ___

**Unscramble the ten letters to find the term.**

The term is: ___ ___ ___ ___ ___ ___ ___ ___ ___ ___

Definition: _____

_____

_____

_____

_____

_____

_____

# Chapter 2 - Facts and Ideas

**Directions:** Identify the incorrect word or term in each of the following statements. Rewrite the sentence to make it correct.

1. The Bill of Rights is our major source of protection for our state rights in the United States.

   Corrected sentence: _____

   _____

2. State courts usually decide whether a particular law violates the Constitution.

   Corrected sentence: _____

   _____

3. The Supreme Court of the United States is made up of twelve justices who decide on important cases.

   Corrected sentence: _____

   _____

   _____

4. The final draft of the Constitution was opposed by a group called the Federalists. This group argued that the Constitution lacked a bill of rights.

   Corrected sentence: _____

   _____

   _____

5. The United States government has one federal government and fifty-one state governments.

   Corrected sentence: _____

   _____

   _____

6. The establishment clause limits the government's power to deprive any person of life, liberty, or property without certain "rules of fair play."

Corrected sentence: _____

_____

_____

7. The separation clause is often called the separation of church and state clause.

Corrected sentence: _____

_____

_____

8. The state government has the right to regulate most business activities in the United States.

Corrected sentence: _____

_____

_____

9. The commerce clause states that government is not supposed to favor or be against any one religion in any way.

Corrected sentence: _____

_____

_____

_____

10. The Eighth Amendment to the Constitution guarantees the right of free speech.

Corrected sentence: _____

_____

_____

# CHAPTER 2 - CRITICAL THINKING ACTIVITY

**A. Directions:** Read each of the following scenarios carefully to determine the rights which were violated. In the blanks provided, state which rights were violated and which Amendment to the Constitution the rights are found in.

1. *Imagine Carlos and Juanita were discussing the upcoming Presidential election. Neither Carlos or Juanita felt the qualifications of the candidates were adequate for the office of President. Carlos and Juanita decided to stage a protest against the election by burning their voter's registration cards in front of city hall. Carlos and Juanita were arrested.*

   The rights which were violated were: _____

   _____

   _____

   Which Amendment? _____

2. *Imagine John was hired by Kreger Security Services as a security guard to work Mondays through Fridays. John had worked for Kreger for two years when they asked him to change his schedule to Tuesdays through Saturdays. John told his superior that he was unable to work on Saturdays because he was Jewish and active in his religion. Kreger fired John because he refused to work on Saturdays.*

   The rights which were violated were: _____

   _____

   _____

   Which Amendment? _____

**B. Directions:** On the writing lines below write two examples of constitutional rights being violated. Be sure to state which rights are being violated and the amendment in which the rights are listed.

1. _____

   _____

   _____

   _____

   _____

   _____

   _____

   _____

   _____

2. _____

   _____

   _____

   _____

   _____

   _____

   _____

   _____

   _____

   _____

12

# CHAPTER 3 - VOCABULARY ACTIVITY

**Directions:** Complete each statement by filling in the blanks with letters of the correct term from this chapter. Then find and circle each key term in the word-search puzzle that follows.

1. Another word for lawsuit is ____ ____ ____ ____ ____ ____ ____ ____ ____ ____.

2. The proper location for a trial to be held is called the ____ ____ ____ ____ ____.

3. The court that reviews the actions of trial courts are called
   ____ ____ ____ ____ ____ ____ ____ ____ ____ courts.

4. A prejudiced belief is known as ____ ____ ____ ____.

5. The court in which facts of a lawsuit are heard and decided is called
   the ____ ____ ____ ____ ____ court.

6. A group of citizens chosen to hear and decide the facts of a case is called
   a ____ ____ ____ ____.

7. ____ ____ ____ ____   ____ ____ ____ ____ is the questioning of potential jurors
   to determine any bias.

8. A trial held before a judge with no jury is a ____ ____ ____ ____ ____ trial.

9. When a case can only be heard in a particular court
   ____ ____ ____ ____ ____ ____ ____ ____ ____ jurisdiction exists.

10. Information presented at the trial, such as photographs, documents, or testimony
    of witnesses is called ____ ____ ____ ____ ____ ____. ____ ____.

11. Geographical divisions of jurisdiction of a federal circuit court of appeals is called
    a judicial ____ ____ ____ ____ ____ ____ ____.

12. A ____ ____ ____ ____ ____ ____ ____ ____ ____ ____ challenge is when
    a prospective juror may be eliminated without cause.

# WORD-SEARCH PUZZLE

```
A  P  P  E  L  L  A  T  E  S  A  Y
I  B  E  N  C  H  L  O  X  O  U  P
R  O  O  R  A  O  P  L  C  V  O  T
A  B  A  R  E  Y  O  A  L  O  L  R
L  A  I  M  O  M  C  I  U  I  V  E
N  R  O  A  T  L  D  R  S  R  P  A
G  O  R  O  S  E  V  T  I  D  J  O
C  I  R  C  U  I  T  O  V  I  U  T
C  O  B  N  O  R  L  E  E  R  R  Y
T  E  E  V  I  D  E  N  C  E  Y  L
O  V  L  I  T  I  G  A  T  I  O  N
```

# CHAPTER 3 - FACTS AND IDEAS

**Directions:** Write a question that corresponds to the answers listed below.

1. Question: _____

_____

_____

Answer:  This is the document that informs someone that a lawsuit has been filed against him or her.

2. Question: _____

_____

_____

Answer:  This juror is exhibiting bias.

3. Question: _____

_____

_____

Answer:  The party may request a review of the trial by an appellate court.

4. Question: _____

_____

_____

Answer:  A diversity of citizenship case exists.

5. Question: _____

_____

_____

Answer:  These are the "judges" in the U. S. Supreme Court.

6. Question: _____

_____

_____

Answer:  It provides a neutral place to go to resolve legal disputes.

7. Question: _____

_____

_____

Answer:  Karen should go to a small claims court.

8. Question: _____

_____

_____

Answer:  Examples are witnesses, photographs, broken locks, etc.

9. Question: _____

_____

_____

Answer:  A change of venue can be requested.

10. Question: _____

_____

_____

Answer:  Minors, convicted criminals, non-citizens, or people who have lived in the state for less than a year.

# CHAPTER 3 - CRITICAL THINKING ACTIVITY

**Directions:** Read the following case to determine the answers to the questions that follow. Provide an explanation for your answers.

Paul was on trial for robbing $100,000 from the Express Bank in Nashville, Tennessee. The teller, whom was held at gunpoint, picked Paul from pictures at the police station. When Paul was arrested in Seattle, Washington, he had a gun and $75,000 in his possession. Paul pleaded innocent. Paul's cousin, Jeremy, told the court that Paul was with him in Seattle on the day of the robbery. Paul's case made the headline every day for three weeks after his arrest. Paul was found guilty.

1. If you were the defense attorney for Paul, what questions would you ask the potential jurors?

_____

_____

_____

_____

_____

_____

_____

2. If Paul did not agree with the decision of the trial, what, if anything, could he do?

_____

_____

_____

_____

3. Is it possible that Paul received an unfair trial? Why or why not?

_____

_____

_____

_____

4. What evidence is possibly against Paul? For Paul?

_____

_____

_____

_____

5. Can the Tennessee courts legally bring Paul to trial in Washington? Why or why not?

_____

_____

_____

_____

6. Can Paul have a bench trial? Why or why not?

_____

_____

_____

_____

# CHAPTER 4 - VOCABULARY ACTIVITY

**Directions:** Match the vocabulary word or term with its proper definition by placing the appropriate letter in the blank.

_____ 1. A crime punishable by a fine or confinement in a local jail

_____ 2. the reason for a criminal act

_____ 3. a threat causing another to commit a crime he or she would not normally commit

_____ 4. unlawful entry into a home with the intent to steal

_____ 5. a serious crime punishable by death

_____ 6. claiming you were someplace else at the time of a crime

_____ 7. determines if the defendant was legally insane at the time of the crime

_____ 8. false signature on a document with intent to defraud

_____ 9. the crime of stealing someone else's car

_____ 10. unlawful and harmful physical contact

_____ 11. threatening another to use harmful force against another

_____ 12. holding someone at gunpoint and stealing money from them

_____ 13. a crime that occurs when an employee steals money from an employer

_____ 14. offering a public official money in lieu of influencing a political decision

_____ 15. voluntarily helping another to commit a crime

A. alibi

B. burglary

C. robbery

D. larceny

E. forgery

F. misdemeanor

G. duress

H. embezzlement

I. battery

J. consent

K. felony

L. bribery

M. M'Naghten test

N. assault

O. motive

# CHAPTER 4 - FACTS AND IDEAS

**Directions:** Read the following examples below to determine whether the act was legal or illegal; a felony, misdemeanor, or a petty offense; and the name of the crime, if there is one. (Example: John broke into Hal's home and stole $500. Answer: Illegal, felony, burglary)

1. Francesca stole a $30.00 pair of earrings from a major department store.

   _____

2. Trey got caught hunting dove on his neighbor's property. His neighbor had "NO TRESPASSING" signs posted.

   _____

3. Sara, who is dying of cancer, asked her niece, Helen, to put her out of her misery by killing her. There were four witnesses present for Sara's request. Helen did what Sara asked.

   _____

4. Jake just robbed Dill's Grocery Store. As Jake is running out of the store and into a car, Dill shoots him. Jake dies.

   _____

5. Debra has four parking tickets from last year that she never paid.

   _____

6. Robert tripped over an object on the sidewalk. While falling his arm hit Josie in the face. It broke Josie's nose.

   _____

7. John walks into his state's senator's office to try to convince him to vote "Yes" on a certain law. To convince the senator John read a list of potential hazards that a "NO" vote would incur.

   _____

8. Dorene sold heroin to teenagers and was caught.

_____

9. Milton loaned you his car for a week. Two days later he reported it missing.

_____

10. Drury, an undercover police officer, pesters Mike every day for a month to buy an ounce of cocaine. Mike finally agrees just to get Drury off his back.

_____

11. Lily threatened you with a baseball bat forcing you to get into her car. She made you drive with her for eight hours while being held against your will.

_____

12. Bruce stole a $10,000 computer from a computer store.

_____

# CHAPTER 4 - CRITICAL THINKING ACTIVITY

**Directions:** Design and write your own stories describing facts in which the following crimes are being committed.

Burglary

_____

_____

_____

_____

_____

_____

Assault

_____

_____

_____

_____

_____

_____

Conspiracy

_____

_____

_____

_____

_____

_____

Embezzlement

_____

_____

_____

_____

_____

_____

Computer crime

_____

_____

_____

_____

_____

_____

# CHAPTER 5 - VOCABULARY ACTIVITY

**Directions:** Complete each sentence with the proper term found in this chapter.

1. Money sought as a remedy for a wrong, such as a tortious act, is called _____.

2. A _____ is a wrongful act for which a court may award damages.

3. A person who commits a tort is called a _____.

4. _____ is an intentional, unexcused act that creates in another a reasonable apprehension or fear of immediate harmful or offensive contact.

5. _____ is harmful or offensive physical contact that intentional and unexcused.

6. Intentional confinement or restraint of another person's movements without justification is _____.

7. Written defamation is _____.

8. Oral defamation is _____.

9. _____ is a misrepresentation of a material fact made knowingly with the intent to deceive another, who is then deceived to his or her detriment, or harm.

10. The unauthorized taking of the personal property of another and the wrongful exercise of the rights of ownership is _____.

11. The _____ person standard is the test to meet to avoid responsibility for negligence.

12. Liability regardless of fault is called _____ liability.

# Chapter 5 - Facts and Ideas

**Directions:** Identify the incorrect term in each of the following statements. Then rewrite the sentence correctly in the blank that follows.

1. Comparative negligence is usually a complete defense to a negligence action.

    _____

    _____

    _____

    _____

2. A store clerk who steals merchandise from the store commits the crime of theft and the crime of conversion.

    _____

    _____

    _____

    _____

3. Trespass to personal property is the wrongful entry onto the real property of another.

    _____

    _____

    _____

    _____

4. The use of a person's name or picture for business purposes without permission is fraud.

    _____

    _____

    _____

    _____

5. Extreme and outrageous intentional behavior that causes severe emotional distress is defamation.

_____

_____

_____

_____

6. Civil wrongs are mostly defined in the statutory law.

_____

_____

_____

_____

7. A crime is a wrongful act for which a court may award damages.

_____

_____

_____

_____

8. An assault is harmful or offensive physical contact that is intentional and unexcused.

_____

_____

_____

_____

# CHAPTER 5 - CRITICAL THINKING ACTIVITY

**Directions:** Design and write your own Legal Focus Problem or Legal Focus Example describing a situation involving each of the following concepts.

1. The tort of assault.

_____

_____

_____

_____

_____

_____

_____

_____

2. The tort of slander

_____

_____

_____

_____

_____

_____

_____

_____

3. Puffery

_____

_____

_____

_____

_____

_____

_____

_____

4. Strict liability

_____

_____

_____

_____

_____

_____

_____

_____

_____

# CHAPTER 6 - VOCABULARY ACTIVITY

**Directions:** Fill in the blank spaces with the vocabulary term that best completes each sentence. Then use the letters in the boxed spaces to form the mystery term. You must unscramble the letters to form the new term. Define the key term.

1. A theory that focuses on which action will generate the greatest good for the greatest number of people is _____.

   ___ ___ ___ ☐ ___ ___ ___ ___ ___ ___ ☐ ___ ☐ ___

2. Standards of fair and honest conduct relating to social behavior is called _____.

   ___ ___ ___ ___ ___ ☐

3. _____ ethics states that individuals should evaluate their actions by considering what would happen if everyone in society performed these actions.

   ___ ___ ___ ☐ ___ ___ ☐

4. Religious principles are an example of _____ ethics.

   ___ ___ ☐ ___ - ___ ___ ___ ☐ ___

5. Corporations should act in a manner which is good for society. This is referred to as a corporation's _____.

   ___ ___ - ___ ☐ ___ ___

   ___ ___ ___ ___ ☐ ___ ___ ___ ___ ___ ___ ___ ___ ☐

6. The seller must be careful of the buyer in a business transaction; this is known as _____.

   ___ ☐ ___ ___ ☐ ___ ___ ___ ___ ___ ☐ ___ ___ ___

7. Using good faith and honesty in business transaction is called _____.

   ☐ __ ☐ __ __ __ __   __ __ __ __ ☐ __

8. Sometimes a person must give up something in order to gain something else.
   This is called a_____.

   __ __ __ __ ☐ - __ ☐ __


**Key Term:** __ __ __ __   __ __ __ __ __ __ __

   __ __ __ __ __ __ __ __


**Definition:**

_____

_____

_____

_____

_____

_____

_____

# CHAPTER 6 - FACTS AND IDEAS

**Directions:** Determine which ethical principle is being violated in each of the following examples and explain your reasoning.

1   Marina was taking a math test and didn't know an answer.  She looked on Dinorah's paper to copy an answer.  Marina felt that it was alright to copy from Dinorah, since she was not harming anyone and she would not pass the class unless she made at least a B on this test.

_____

_____

_____

_____

_____

_____

_____

_____

2.   Cathy, a salesperson, was trying to meet her quota of sales in the ladies department store of Sala's.  Even though she knew that the clearance items were nonrefundable she told her customers that they could return the clearance items that they bought that day.

_____

_____

_____

_____

_____

_____

_____

_____

3. John rents apartments to retiree's for $400 a month. Although he makes a profit on the rent, he would like to make more money so that he can quit his part-time job as a janitor and pay his employees more money. Even though he knows that his tenants are on a fixed income and a few of them would probably have problems coming up with the extra $100 per month, he decides to raise the rent to $500 per month. He realizes that the apartments are not even worth $500, but most tenants probably will not leave, since they have lived there for more than 20 years.

_____

_____

_____

_____

_____

_____

_____

4. Dave was a lender for The Bank of Orlando. Jason and Roberta Simms were desperately trying to take out a loan to save their business. The Bank of Orlando normally charges 8% for such a loan, but Dave knew that since the Simms' were desperate, he could charge them 9%; therefore making more money for him and The Bank of Orlando.

_____

_____

_____

_____

_____

_____

_____

© West Educational Publishing

Name_____ Date_____

# CHAPTER 6 - CRITICAL THINKING ACTIVITY

Braxton Electronics, a major soft drink manufacturer in Atlanta, Georgia was asked to sponsor a Special Olympics to benefit disabled children on Labor Day weekend. Braxton agreed. Peter Kanston, an employee who was responsible for planning the event, decided that Braxton could make a profit from the event by charging spectators an entrance fee of $2.00 each. Peter also decided to set up a refreshment stand in which they would contribute 50% of the profit to the disabled children's fund. On the day of the event, Braxton made $10,000 from entrance fees and $3,000 from the refreshments. They donated $1,500 to the disabled children's fund.

1. Was Braxton involved in any unethical acts? Explain.

   _____

   _____

   _____

   _____

2. Rewrite this story so that the outcome shows Braxton exhibiting social responsibility in a more favorable light.

   _____

   _____

   _____

   _____

   _____

   _____

   _____

   _____

   _____

   _____

   _____

# CHAPTER 7 - VOCABULARY ACTIVITY

**Directions:** Complete each sentence with the appropriate vocabulary term found in this chapter.

1. People involved in contracts rely on _____
   _____, the honesty and thoughtfulness, of the other person.

2. A _____ is a legal agreement to do or not do a specified thing.

3. _____ is something of value promised or received to make a contract legal.

4. A contract which can be revoked before an act is performed is called a/n _____  _____.

5. If a contract is stated in oral and written form it is referred to as a/n _____  _____.

6. A contract in which both parties exchange promises is a/n _____
   _____.

7. A contract created by law to prevent a tragedy, but not made by mutual agreement of the parties is known as a _____ contract.

8. A contract formed by unspoken conduct is called a/n _____
   _____  _____ contract.

9. A bail bond in a criminal matter is an example of a _____ bond. This occurs when someone agrees to pay a sum of money if a certain event occurs.

10. Most contracts do not require a special form to be considered valid. This is known as a/n _____ contract.

11. A contract which has not yet been fully performed is known as a/n _____ contract.

12. A contract in which one party has a legal right to cancel is called a/n
_____ contract.

13. A contract that was made orally, but by law must be in writing is known as
a/n _____ contract.

14. An agreement, such as one made to buy illegal drugs, is considered
a _____ contract.

15. A contract which has been successfully completed by both parties is called a/n
_____ contract.

**Define:** objective theory of contracts

_____

_____

_____

_____

_____

# CHAPTER 7 - FACTS AND IDEAS

**Directions:** Write short answers for each of the following questions. You may use your book to find the answers.

1. Explain the relationship between the promisor and the promisee.

_____

_____

_____

2. Define the term "goods". List some examples.

_____

_____

_____

3. Name three possible defenses to the formation of a contract that could make the contract invalid.

A. _____

B. _____

C. _____

4. Explain the difference between a unilateral and a bilateral contract.

_____

_____

_____

5. Joan says to Miguel, "I'll give your $50 for your bicycle." Who is the offeror and who is the offeree?

_____

_____

_____

6. Are both an agreement and consideration necessary in order to form a contract? Explain.

_____

_____

_____

7. What is the difference between an express contract and an implied contract?

_____

_____

_____

_____

8. What is the importance of the objective theory of contracts?

_____

_____

_____

_____

9. Why were the quasi contracts created by law?

_____

_____

_____

10. Define and give an example of an informal contract.

_____

_____

_____

_____

11. Why is a voidable contract not considered a void contract?

_____

_____

_____

_____

12. State an example of an executory contract.

_____

_____

_____

_____

# CHAPTER 7 - CRITICAL THINKING ACTIVITY

Joe, 22, offered to sell his record collection to Emanuel, 16, for $100. Emanuel agreed to pay Joe the $100 in two days.

1. Was a contract made?

   _____

2. What type of contract is this an example of?

   _____

3. Is this contract void? Why or why not?

   _____

   _____

4. Is this contract voidable? Why or why not?

   _____

   _____

Rewrite this story to make it a unilateral contract.

_____

_____

_____

_____

_____

_____

_____

_____

_____

Selena paid Bruce $200 for a painting that he told her was a Picasso original. She found out a week later that the painting was actually an imitation, worth only $30.

5. What type of contract was made?

_____

6. Is this contract void? Why or why not?

_____

_____

7. Is this contract voidable? Why or why not?

_____

_____

_____

Rewrite this story to make it a valid contract.

_____

_____

_____

_____

_____

_____

_____

_____

_____

_____

Tomer offers Jesse $50 if Jesse helps him sell his home.

8.  What type of contract is this?

    _____

9.  Is Tomer legally bound to this contract?  Why or why not?

    _____

    _____

Rewrite this story to make it a bilateral contract.

_____

_____

_____

_____

_____

_____

_____

_____

_____

_____

# CHAPTER 8 - VOCABULARY ACTIVITY

**Directions:** Choose eight of the following terms from the list below. Define and give an example of each term you choose.

| | |
|---|---|
| acceptance | agreement |
| counteroffer | firm offer |
| invitation to negotiate | mailbox rule |
| mirror-image rule | offer |
| revocation | unequivocal acceptance |

1. Term: _____

   Definition: _____

   _____

   Example: _____

   _____

2. Term: _____

   Definition: _____

   _____

   Example: _____

   _____

3. Term: _____

   Definition: _____

   _____

   Example: _____

   _____

4. Term: _____

   Definition: _____

   _____

   Example: _____

   _____


5. Term: _____

   Definition: _____

   _____

   Example: _____

   _____


6. Term: _____

   Definition: _____

   _____

   Example: _____

   _____


7. Term: _____

   Definition: _____

   _____

   Example: _____

   _____


8. Term: _____

   Definition: _____

   _____

   Example: _____

   _____

# CHAPTER 8 - FACTS AND IDEAS

**Directions:** Read each of the following scenarios to determine if a contract exists. Then tell why or why not the contract is valid.

1. Samuel states, "I hate this old lawn mower. Some day I'm going to sell it for $10.00." Nathan hands Samuel a $10.00 bill and says, "I'll take it."

A. Does a contract exist? _____

B. Why or why not?_____

_____

_____

2. Eileen posted a flyer in her apartment complex that read, **"LIKE NEW — BLUE SOFA FOR ONLY $50.00"**. She received three calls for the offer.

A. Does a contract exist? _____

B. Why or why not?_____

_____

_____

3. On Monday, Allen agreed to repair Margot's sink for $100. Upon leaving Allen's home, Margot said, "See you tomorrow at 2:00". Allen did not arrive at Margot's home until 4:00.

A. Does a contract exist? _____

B. Why or why not?_____

_____

_____

4. Juan purchased a new 486 DX computer. While he and his friend, Maria, were hooking it up, he broke one of the cables and shouted, "I'll sell you this piece of junk for 20 bucks." Maria said, "Okay," and grabbed her purse to write Juan a check.

A. Does a contract exist? _____

B. Why or why not?_____

_____

_____

5. Mary Ann offers to sell her onyx ring to Betty for $50.00. Betty says, "I'll buy the ring for $35.00".

A. Does a contract exist? _____

B. Why or why not?_____

_____

_____

6. On Monday, Terry mailed Michael an offer to buy her computer for $500. Michael accepted the offer and mailed the acceptance letter on Wednesday. On Thursday, however, Terry changed her mind and mailed a revocation to Michael, which he received Thursday.

A. Does a contract exist? _____

B. Why or why not?_____

_____

_____

7. Buddy offers Trisha $200 for her car. Trisha accepts and agreed to deliver the car on Friday. On Thursday, Trisha had an accident which totaled her car.

A. Does a contract exist? _____

B. Why or why not?_____

_____

_____

48

# CHAPTER 8 - CRITICAL THINKING ACTIVITY

**Directions:** Read the following scenario and answer the questions that follow.

Ramone places an ad in Monday's local newspaper advertising the sale of his dalmatian puppy for $100, to be paid on delivery. Ramone receives three phone calls from the ad on Tuesday. His first call was from Susie who said, "I'll give your $75 for the puppy." His second caller was from Barbara who offered $100, but would pay Ramone next week, on the condition that the dog checks out at the veterinarian. His final caller was from Bernice, who agreed to pay Ramone $100 on Friday when she came to pick up the puppy.

1.  Is Ramone obligated to all of these people? Why or why not?

    _____

    _____

2.  Is there a contract with Susie? Why or why not?

    _____

    _____

3.  Is there a contract with Barbara? Why or why not?

    _____

    _____

4.  Is there a contract with Bernice: Why or why not?

    _____

    _____

5.  If Bernice received a letter in the mail from Ramone on Thursday revoking his offer, would the revocation be valid? Why or why not?

    _____

    _____

    _____

    _____

# CHAPTER 9 - VOCABULARY ACTIVITY

**Directions:** Fill in the blank with the appropriate vocabulary term from this chapter. Then fill in the appropriate letter that corresponds with the numbers in the puzzle to solve the mystery term.

1.  The unmaking of a contract by returning both parties to their original positions is called _____.

    ___ ___ ___ ___ ___ ___ ___ ___ ___
           6

2.  A promise to do what one is already required to do is a _____ duty.

    ___ ___ ___ ___ ___ ___ ___ ___ ___ ___ ___
             5

3.  Value given in return for a promise is called _____.

    ___ ___ ___ ___ ___ ___ ___ ___ ___ ___ ___ ___ ___
      3

4.  A promise to reward someone for an action that took place before the promise was made is called _____.

    ___ ___ ___ ___
        9

    ___ ___ ___ ___ ___ ___ ___ ___ ___ ___ ___ ___ ___

5.  The relinquishing of a right is called a _____.

    ___ ___ ___ ___ ___ ___ ___
        8

6.  A contract in which the seller agrees to sell and the buyer agrees to purchase all of something the seller produces is called a/n _____ contract.

    ___ ___ ___ ___ ___ ___
       1

7. The legal right to contract is known as _____ _____.

____ ___ ____ ___ ___ ___ ___ ___ ___ ___ ___
                                                                         10

____ ___ - ___ ___ ___ ___ ___ ___
                                  10

8. Refraining from doing something one has a legal right to do is called _____.

____ ___ ___ ___ ___ ___ ___ ___ ___ ___ ___
          2

9. A promise given without anything expected in return is considered a _____.

____ ___ ___ ___

10. A legal cost is referred to as a legal _____.

____ ___ ___ ___ ___ ___ ___ ___ ___
                                 4

## Key Term:

____ ___ ___ ___ ___ ___ ___ ___ ___ ___
 1    2    3    4    6    5    5    3    2    7

____ ___ ___ ___ ___ ___ ___ ___
 8    5    9    3    1    1    8   10

## Define the Key Term:

_____

_____

_____

_____

_____

# CHAPTER 9 - FACTS AND IDEAS

**Directions:** Read each of the following cases to determine if there is a contract. State your reasoning.

1. Mary offered Paul $10,000 if he agreed to attend college. Paul had just been accepted to UCLA and had already registered.
   Is there a contract? Why or why not?

   _____

   _____

   _____

2. Daniel told Sally that he would give her $500 because she was his favorite niece. Sally said, "I accept."
   Is there a contract? Why or why not?

   _____

   _____

   _____

3. Vivian offered Jake $250 if he agreed not to go to Hawaii on vacation. Jake did not go because of the offer.
   Is there a contract? Why or why not?

   _____

   _____

   _____

4. Susan's Uncle Tom offered her $500 per month for a year if she did not take a job offer that would place her 1,000 miles away from her family. Susan declined the job because of the agreement.
   Is there a contract? Why or why not?

   _____

   _____

   _____

5. Bob's cousin, Ted, was a computer salesman. Ted was able to get Bob a bargain on a computer, saving Bob $600. After the computer was installed, Bob told Ted that he was going to give Ted $200 for helping him get the discount.
Is there a contract? Why or why not?

_____

_____

_____

6. Peter and Azele had ordered their third beer together when Peter offered Azele $15,000 for his new car. The car was worth $20,000. Azele agreed.
Is there a contract? Why or why not?

_____

_____

_____

7. Pedro owed Camille $400. One day Camille ran into Pedro and said, "Where is my $400?" Pedro exclaimed, "All I have is $300." Camille agreed to take it. Can Camille sue Pedro for the remaining $100?
Why or why not?

_____

_____

_____

8. Jared offered Cindy $1,000 if she quit smoking for a year. After a year of no cigarettes, Cindy called Jared for the $1,000.
Is there a contract? Why or why not?

_____

_____

_____

# CHAPTER 9 - CRITICAL THINKING ACTIVITY

**Directions:** Choose two of the concepts below and write your own Legal Focus example or Legal Focus problem that will help to explain the concept.

a. **forbearance** — refraining from or promising to refrain from doing something one has a legal right to do.

b. **past consideration** — a promise to reward someone for actions or events that took place before the promise to reward.

c. **requirements contract** — a contract in which the buyer agrees to purchase from the seller, and the seller agrees to sell to the buyer, all of some good the buyer requires.

d. **promissory estoppel** — enforcing a contract unsupported by consideration if it is an important promise, and one upon which another relies on to his or her detriment.

1. Legal Focus

_____

_____

_____

_____

_____

_____

_____

_____

_____

_____

2. Legal Focus

_____

_____

_____

_____

_____

_____

_____

_____

# CHAPTER 10 - VOCABULARY ACTIVITY

**Directions:** Complete each sentence by filling in the blanks with key terms found in this chapter. Then find and circle each term in the word search exercise that follows.

1. Charging an illegal interest rate is called _____.

   ____ ____ ____ ____ ____

2. If you have a real economic risk in a person or property, you have _____ interest.

   ____ ____ ____ ____ ____ ____ ____ ____ ____

3. Laws restricting business activities on Sunday are called _____ laws.

   ____ ____ ____ ____

4. A car loan in which you pay $200 per month for four years is called a/n _____ loan.

   ____ ____ ____ ____ ____ ____ ____ ____ ____ ____ ____

5. When two parties to a contract forget to include the rate of interest in the contract, the _____ rate of interest will be used.

   ____ ____ ____ ____ ____

6. When you must pay something for only a chance to win a certain property, this is called _____.

   ____ ____ ____ ____ ____ ____ ____ ____

7. A grossly unfair contract is considered _____.

   ____ ____ ____ ____ ____ ____ ____ ____ ____ ____ ____ ____

8. A true objective meeting of the minds is referred to as _____.

   ____ ____ ____ ____ ____ ____ ____   ____ ____ ____ ____ ____ ____

9. A mistake made by both parties to a contract about the same material fact is a _____ mistake.

___ ___ ___ ___ ___ ___ ___ ___ ___

10. Threat of or actual physical harm to coerce someone into a contract is _____.

___ ___ ___ ___ ___ ___

11. Damages paid to set an example for similar wrongdoers are called _____ damages.

___ ___ ___ ___ ___ ___ ___ ___

12. If a seller knowingly misleads the buyer of a material fact by his or her actions, this is called misrepresentation by _____.

___ ___ ___ ___ ___ ___ ___

## WORD PUZZLE

```
P O L I D O W G J O G L
I N A N T U L S O N E O
N S W H A N R H E R N T
I I E S O C E E Y Z U C
N D V O P O O L S V I U
S U I E U N I D C S N D
U G T S O S M I T C E N
R A I R L C U E N S A O
A M N B A I O R C K S C
B B U R R O L I Y K S A
L L P O E N G S O O E R
E I N S T A L L M E N T
R N B E A B L I E V T A
O G U T L L L E G A L E
L O H S I E R U T E O R
```

# CHAPTER 10 - FACTS AND IDEAS

**Directions:** Find the incorrect word or term in each statement and rewrite the sentence to make it correct.

1. Federal Savings Bank charged Harold the judgement rate of interest because they forgot to fix the rate of interest on his contract.

_____

_____

_____

_____

2. John was having a Super Bowl party on Sunday; however, he could not buy the alcoholic beverages on Sunday because of his state's usury laws.

_____

_____

_____

_____

3. Sal wanted Jose' to sign an unconscionable clause so that Sal would not be responsible for Jose's injuries if he were hurt when building his garage.

_____

_____

_____

_____

4. Toby was attending Sinbad's garage sale. When Toby asked Sinbad how much he wanted for the wheelbarrow, Sinbad replied, "I'll take $15.00." When Toby paid for the wheelbarrow, Sinbad wrote a receipt for $10.00. Toby did not notice and walked away. A bilateral mistake was made here.

_____

_____

_____

_____

5. Quinton committed fraud. The plaintiff was awarded compensatory damages to set an example for other wrongdoers.

_____

_____

_____

_____

6. Susan committed duress when she convinced her sick aunt to sell her $100,000 home to Susan for $25,000 or she wouldn't take care of her any more.

_____

_____

_____

_____

7. Mirabella could not legally take out a life insurance policy on her friend, Tricia, because she had no undue influence.

_____

_____

_____

_____

8. Tomeka violated the blue laws when she sold tickets for a drawing to win a new television set.

_____

_____

_____

_____

9. Nicholas bought an automobile in which he paid 10% interest for four years. His payments were $250 per month. This was a usury loan.

_____

_____

_____

_____

10. Beth signed an exculpatory contract when the lender charged her 25% over the legal rate of interest.

_____

_____

_____

_____

# CHAPTER 10 - CRITICAL THINKING ACTIVITY

**Directions:** Read the cases below and answer the questions that follow.

1. Jim wanted to sell his speed boat to Rochelle. When Rochelle went to Jim's home to inspect it, she offered him $6,200. Jim accepted. The following day Jim typed a letter to Rochelle with the offer. While typing the amount, he mistakenly typed $2,600 instead of $6,200. When Rochelle received the letter and realized the mistake, she exclaimed, "Too bad — it is in writing."

A. What type of mistake was made by Jim?

_____

B. Is this contract enforceable? Why or why not?

_____

_____

2. Clifton went to United Bank to take out a loan for a used car. Since Clifton's credit was not very good, the loan officer charged Clifton 15% interest on the loan, which was 5% higher than the average car loan. Clifton said that he was going to sue the bank for charging usury rates.

A. Was Clifton correct? Why or why not?

_____

_____

_____

B. What would happen if the loan officer charged Clifton 20% on the loan?

_____

C. What would happen if the loan officer charged Clifton 40% on the loan?

_____

3. Write your own case showing an example of *misrepresentation by silence.*

_____

_____

_____

_____

_____

_____

_____

_____

_____

_____

_____

63

# CHAPTER 11 - VOCABULARY ACTIVITY

**Directions:** Define each of the following terms and then write a sentence using the term to show that you understand the concept.

1. Statute of Frauds

   Definition: _____

   _____

   _____

   Sentence: _____

   _____

   _____

2. Cosign

   Definition: _____

   _____

   _____

   Sentence: _____

   _____

   _____

3. Lease

   Definition: _____

   _____

   _____

   Sentence: _____

   _____

   _____

4. The One-Year Rule
   Definition: _____

   _____

   _____

   Sentence: _____

   _____

   _____

5. Mortgage

   Definition: _____

   _____

   _____

   Sentence: _____

   _____

   _____

6. Memorandum
   Definition: _____

   _____

   _____

   Sentence: _____

   _____

   _____

7. Parol evidence rule
   Definition: _____

   _____

   _____

   Sentence: _____

   _____

   _____

8. Plain meaning rule

   Definition: _____

   _____

   _____

   Sentence: _____

   _____

   _____

9. Prenuptial agreement

   Definition: _____

   _____

   _____

   Sentence: _____

   _____

   _____

10. Integrated contract

    Definition: _____

    _____

    _____

    Sentence: _____

    _____

    _____

# CHAPTER 11 - FACTS AND IDEAS

**Directions:** Read the following situations to decide whether the contract stated must be in writing under the Statute of Frauds. State your reasoning.

1. Stella told Jerome that she would sell her car to him for $750.

   Is a writing required for this contract? _____

   because _____

   _____

2. Hope was purchasing a $350 refrigerator for her first apartment. She told the salesperson that her mother would pay for it if she could not. When the salesperson telephoned Hopes's mother, Cathy, to confirm payment, Cathy agreed to pay if Hope could not.

   Is a writing required in order for Cathy to be responsible? _____

   because _____

   _____

3. Jenny and Keith were about to be married. Keith owned a very profitable business. One night as they were discussing their wedding plans, Keith asked Jenny to promise him that in the event that they divorced, she would not try to claim anything from his business. Jenny promised she would not.

   Is a writing required to enforce Jenny's promise? _____

   because _____

   _____

4. Louise borrowed $800 from Ronda. Louise took a piece of notebook paper and wrote, "On this 16th day of November 1993, I agree to pay Ronda Brooks $800 on January 1, 1994. Then Louise signed her name.

   Is this writing sufficient? _____

   because _____

   _____

5. Susan agreed to sell Danny her motorcycle for $450. When Danny picked up the motorcycle he told Susan he would mail her a check next week. Danny never sent the check.

Is this contract required to be in writing _____

because _____

_____

6. Gina orally contracts to sell a 1/8 acre lot to Richard for $475. One week later, Gina decides not to sell.

Can Richard enforce the contract this contract? _____

because _____

_____

7. Jim orally agrees to lease his apartment to Jackie for eighteen months. After six months, Jackie moves out. Jim told Jackie that she owes him money for the twelve months that the apartment was vacant.

Can Jim enforce this contract? _____

because _____

_____

8. Evelyn agreed to sell her car to Millie for $2,500. While negotiating the price, Millie asked Evelyn if she would agree to put new tires on the car and have the car painted. Evelyn agreed. They both signed the contract which stated the amount agreed upon and that Evelyn would put new tires on the car.

Is Millie legally entitled to a paint job? _____

because _____

_____

# CHAPTER 11 - CRITICAL THINKING ACTIVITY

**Directions:** Read the case and answer the questions that follow.

Paul agreed to build an attached screened lanai to the back of Merry's house. While negotiating the contract, Merry agreed to pay $4,500 for the lanai if Paul agreed to include carpeting. Paul agreed. When the contract was written up the only term in addition to building the lanai was that Paul would paint the outside of the lanai. Before signing the contract, Merry convinced Paul to do the work for $4,000. With a ballpoint pen, Merry drew a line through the $4,500 and wrote in $4,000 above it. Then they both signed the contract.

1. Must this contract be in writing? _____
   Why or why not?

   _____

   _____

2. Can Paul be legally responsible for carpeting the lanai? _____
   Why or why not?

   _____

   _____

3. Is the pen writing in which Merry crosses out the original amount before signing the contract enforceable? _____
   Why or why not?

   _____

   _____

4. What could Merry have done with the contract to better protect herself?

   _____

   _____

   _____

   _____

   _____

   _____

# Chapter 12 - Vocabulary Activity

**Directions:** Fill in the blanks with the appropriate vocabulary term found in this chapter. Then solve the puzzle by writing the letter that corresponds with the number in the blank to the one in the puzzle.

1. The termination of one's contractual obligation is called a/n _____.

   __ __ __ __ __ __ __ __ __
          1

2. The transfer of a right to a third person is a/n _____.

   __ __ __ __ __ __ __ __ __ __
          2

3. The transfer of a duty to a third person is a/n _____.

   __ __ __ __ __ __ __ __ __ __
          3

4. A person who receives benefits from a contract is known as the _____.

   __ __ __ __ __ __ __ __ __ __ __
        5        9

5. The designated beneficiary on a life insurance policy is known as the _____ beneficiary.

   __ __ __ __ __ __ __ __
      11

6. Fulfilling one's obligation under a contract is known as _____.

   __ __ __ __ __ __ __ __ __ __ __
        7

7. When parties to a contract discharge their obligations by performing their duties as stated in the contract, this is called _____ performance.

   __ __ __ __ __ __
       4

8. When a party to a contract earnestly performs most, but not all, of the elements of the contract, this is _____ performance.

\_\_\_\_ \_\_\_\_ \_\_\_\_ \_\_\_\_ \_\_\_\_ \_\_\_\_ \_\_\_\_ \_\_\_\_ \_\_\_\_ \_\_\_\_ \_\_\_\_

9. Failure to perform part or all of the required duties under a contract is a/n _____.

\_\_\_\_ \_\_\_\_ \_\_\_\_ \_\_\_\_ \_\_\_\_ \_\_\_\_
             12

10. A _____ substitutes a new party for one of the original parties to the contract.

\_\_\_\_ \_\_\_\_ \_\_\_\_ \_\_\_\_ \_\_\_\_ \_\_\_\_ \_\_\_\_ \_\_\_\_

11. An agreement to perform an act to satisfy an existing contractual duty is a/n _____.

\_\_\_\_ \_\_\_\_ \_\_\_\_ \_\_\_\_ \_\_\_\_ \_\_\_\_
       8

12. The _____ _____ doctrine applies when performance of the contract would be dramatically more difficult or more expensive than expected.

\_\_\_\_ \_\_\_\_ \_\_\_\_ \_\_\_\_ \_\_\_\_ \_\_\_\_ \_\_\_\_ \_\_\_\_ \_\_\_\_ \_\_\_\_

\_\_\_\_ \_\_\_\_ \_\_\_\_ \_\_\_\_ \_\_\_\_ \_\_\_\_ \_\_\_\_ \_\_\_\_ \_\_\_\_ \_\_\_\_ \_\_\_\_ \_\_\_\_ \_\_\_\_ \_\_\_\_ \_\_\_\_ \_\_\_\_ \_\_
                                            10

**Term:**   \_\_\_ \_\_\_ \_\_\_ \_\_\_ \_\_\_ \_\_\_ \_\_\_ \_\_\_ \_\_\_ \_\_\_ \_\_\_ \_\_\_
     3   2   4   5   1   5   6   3   4   7   8   9

       \_\_\_ \_\_\_ \_\_\_ \_\_\_ \_\_\_ \_\_\_
      10   8  11   3   1  12

**Define the term:** _____

_____

_____

_____

# CHAPTER 12 - FACT AND IDEAS

**Directions:** Read each situation carefully. Then answer the questions which follow.

1. Janice takes out a life insurance policy with Booker Insurance Company on her husband, Michael, for $10,000.

A. Who is the beneficiary?_____

B. Can Janice legally do this? Why or why not? _____

_____

_____

2. Joe hires Miguel to paint his car for $200. Miguel breaks his arm and asks Joe if Tony, his partner, can paint the car instead. Joe agrees.

A. What kind of transfer has occurred? _____

_____

B. Is this legal? _____

C. In this case, what term is used to refer to Joe's role? _____

D. What term refers to Miguel's role?_____

E. What term refers to Tony's role? _____

3. Clarese owes Beth $200. However, Beth wants to buy a stereo from Derek for $200. Beth tells Clarese to pay the $200 she owes her to Derek. Clarese paid Derek.

A. Can Beth legally do this? _____

B. What kind of transfer occurred? _____

_____

C. What term refers to Clarese's role in this case? _____

D. What term refers to Beth's role? _____

E. What term refers to Derek's role? _____

4. The county of Hillsborough contracted with Nelson Painting Services to paint house numbers on the curbs of all of the urban homes in Hillsborough County.

A. What term refers to Hillsborough County's role in this case? _____

B. What term refers to Nelson Painting Services role? _____

_____

C. Who is the incidental beneficiary? _____

_____

D. Can Nelson Painting Services delegate their duties to Prism Painting Company?

_____

_____

E. What is it called if Nelson Printing Services paints the numbers on the curb white, instead of yellow, as the contract expressed?_____

_____

5. Dell signed a contract with Carrie to repair her computer. The day before Dell was supposed to work on Carrie's computer, he contracted the flu. Carrie told Dell that she needed it repaired this week. Dell and Carrie both agreed to cancel the contract so that Carrie could hire someone else.

A. Is this legal? _____

B. What is this called? _____

_____

C. What is the term that refers to Dell's role in this case? _____

_____

D. What is the term that refers to Carrie's role in this case? _____

_____

# CHAPTER 12 - CRITICAL THINKING ACTIVITY

**Directions:** Read the following cases and answer the questions that follow.

1. Anton hired Polly to paint a portrait of Anton's family. Anton hired Polly because she was known world-wide for her exceptional skills in painting. After three weeks of working on the portrait, which was only half done, Polly was in a bad accident and became paralyzed. Polly was physically unable to complete the portrait. Anton was furious.

A. Can Polly delegate her duties to Sergio? Why or why not?

_____

_____

B. Can Anton sue Polly? Why or why not?

_____

_____

C. Is this an example of substantial performance? Why or why not?

_____

_____

D. Suggest ways in which Anton could be satisfied?

_____

_____

E. If Polly had not been in an accident, but simply did not want to complete the portrait because of the large amount of time that it was taking to complete the portrait, how would the situation change for Polly?

_____

_____

F. How would the situation change for Anton?

_____

_____

# CHAPTER 13 - VOCABULARY ACTIVITY

**Directions:** Match the appropriate term with its definition.

_____ 1. money sought as a remedy for a breach of contract

_____ 2. small money award granted to plaintiff who suffered a wrong but no actual loss

_____ 3. rule that requires plaintiff to reduce the damages

_____ 4. an equitable remedy to cancel a contract

_____ 5. remedy that requires performance of the act promised in the contract

_____ 6. an intentional giving up of a legal right

_____ 7. an amount specified ina contract to be paid upon default or breach of contract

_____ 8. the court rewrites a contract to reflect the parties' true intentions

_____ 9. damages that punish the defendant

_____ 10. failure to perform the duties under a contract

_____ 11. compensation for the actual loss of the bargain caused by a breach of contract

_____ 12. relief given to the innocent party when the other party has breached a contract

A. rescission

B. reformation

C. damages

D. breach

E. nominal damages

F. remedy

G. mitigate

H. general damages

I. waiver

J. specific performance

K. exemplary damages

L. penalty

# CHAPTER 13 - FACTS AND IDEAS

**Directions:** Read each statement to determine which type of damages would probably be awarded if the innocent party sued. Place the appropriate letter in the blank.

G = general damages
C = consequential damages
P = punitive damages
N = nominal damages
L = liquidated damages
S = specific performance

_____ 1. Gill did not get the cooling element to Herman's Meats at the time he promised. Herman lost $1,200 worth of meat because of not having the cooling element.

_____ 2. Robert had to pay Bella $200 because of a provision in their contract stating that $50 per day would be paid for every day the pool was late in completion.

_____ 3. Sue breached her contract with Chuck to buy his computer. However, Chuck found another buyer the next day, willing to pay $150 more than Sue agreed to pay.

_____ 4. Larry breached a contract he had with Shelia. He decided he did not want to sell her the one-acre lot that he promised to sell her.

_____ 5. John orally agreed to sell his car to Dawn for $350. John breached. Two days later Dawn found another car for $400.

_____ 6. Simon committed fraud while selling an expensive painting to Clarence. In court, Clarence was awarded his initial payment for the painting. The judge also awarded Clarence damages to teach Simon a lesson. What are these damages called?

_____ 7. Debra contracted with Charmaine to buy Charmaine's one-of-a-kind antique 1800's pearl ring. At the last minute, Charmaine decided not to sell the ring to Debra because she wanted it for herself.

_____ 8. Elliot Enterprises contracted with Allen to write computer programs for their company during the holiday season. Elliot Enterprises agreed to pay Allen $3,000 for November and December. Elliot canceled the contract in mid-November. Allen could not find another job until January.

_____ 9. Toyland contracts with RJ Industries to deliver their holiday inventory of dolls by November 20. Toyland tells RJ that it is imperative that they receive the order before December, their biggest sale month of the year. RJ does not deliver the dolls until December 27.

_____10. Sean contracts with Alfred to buy apples at $1.00 per pound. Alfred breaches and never delivers the apples. The next day, Sean found the apples for 90 cents per pound.

# CHAPTER 13 - CRITICAL THINKING ACTIVITY

**Directions:** Read the case below and answer the questions that follow.

The Brooks' contracted with Genoa Construction to build their dream house. The Brooks' agreed to pay Genoa $95,000 for the home. A clause was put into the contract in which Genoa agreed to pay the Brooks' $100 per day if the job was not finished by the end of the year. The contract specified that the kitchen cabinets were to be a solid light oak and the kitchen floor would be of Italian tile. When the Brooks' inspected the kitchen after completion, they found that the cabinets were a medium color solid oak and the kitchen floor was vinyl. When the house was completed on January 8, the Brooks' decided to sue Genoa.

1. What type of damages could the Brooks' sue for because of the late completion date? How much could they receive in damages?

   _____

   _____

2. What type of damages could the Brooks' sue for because of the cabinets? How much could they receive in damages?

   _____

   _____

3. What type of damages could the Brooks' sue for because of the vinyl floor? How much could they receive in damages?

   _____

   _____

4. If the Brooks' decided to accept the breach concerning the cabinets, what term would describe this act of acceptance?

   _____

   _____

# CHAPTER 14 - VOCABULARY ACTIVITY

**Directions:** Complete each sentence with the proper term found in this chapter. Then complete the puzzle with the corresponding letter to solve the new term.

1. Property that has no physical value, such as stocks and bonds are called _____ properties.

   ___ ___ ___ ___ ___ ___ ___ ___ ___ ___
                          1

2. The formal right of ownership to property is a _____.

   ___ ___ ___ ___ ___
    7

3. A person who regularly deals in goods in which he or she is very knowledgeable about is a/n _____.

   ___ ___ ___ ___ ___ ___ ___ ___
           3

4. An offer for the sale of goods made in writing and signed by the merchant is a/n _____ offer.

   ___ ___ ___ ___
     11

5. The way parties conduct themselves toward each other after a contract is created is called _____ _____ _____

   ___ ___ ___ ___ ___ ___    ___ ___

   ___ ___ ___ ___ ___ ___ ___ ___ ___ ___ ___
    9                  6

6. A grossly unfair contract is a/n _____ contract.

   ___ ___ ___ ___ ___ ___ ___ ___ ___ ___ ___ ___ ___
     2

7. The carrier's signed receipt of the goods which serves as a contract during the transportation of the goods is a _____ _____ _____.

___ ___ ___ ___ ___ ___ ___ ___ ___ ___ ___ ___
                                           5

8. A transaction in which the owner of the goods gives another authority to sell the goods is a/n _____.

___ ___ ___ ___ ___ ___ ___ ___ ___ ___
            13

9. The actions and communications that take place between the parties before the agreement is made is referred to as the _____ _____ _____.

___ ___ ___ ___ ___ ___ ___ ___ ___ ___ ___ ___ ___ ___ ___
         10                               8

10. Specifying which good is the subject matter of the contract before the contract is made is called _____.

___ ___ ___ ___ ___ ___ ___ ___ ___ ___ ___ ___ ___
                4

11. A common business practice in a place, vocation, or trade is called _____ _____ _____.

___ ___ ___ ___ ___ ___ ___ ___ ___ ___ ___
         14

12. A sales contract in which the seller is responsible for delivering the goods to a carrier is called a/n _____ _____.

___ ___ ___ ___ ___ ___ ___ ___ ___ ___ ___ ___ ___ ___ ___ ___ ___
       12

**TERM:** ___ ___ ___ ___ ___ ___ ___ ___ ___
      1    2    2    5     4    6    8    7    12

        ___ ___ ___ ___ ___ ___ ___ ___ ___
      9   10   11   3   12   6   13   14   11

**DEFINITION OF TERM:** _____

_____

_____

82

# CHAPTER 14 - FACTS AND IDEAS

**Directions:** Explain why the following people are mistaken in their understanding of the sale.

1. Ricardo, an accountant, was moving to a new home and decided to have a garage sale. Michael bought Ricardo's lawn mower for $30 at the garage sale. One week later, Michael brought back the mower to Ricardo and demanded his money back because the mower didn't have a sharp blade on it. Michael told Ricardo that he was responsible for the mower because he sold it.

   Michael is wrong because _____

   _____

   _____

2. Herschel signed a contract with Acme Tires to buy all of the tires he sells from Acme for one year. When Acme didn't produce any tires for a week, Herschel called the Sales Manager of Acme and told him that he wanted to cancel his output contract.

   Herschel is wrong because _____

   _____

   _____

3. Jessica owed Selena $800. Selena wrote on a piece of stationery, "I, Jessica Stall, owe Selena Pierce $800, payable on March 2, 1994." Selena then dated and signed the paper. Jessica telephoned Selena two months later and said, "I can not pay the $800. Besides, that piece of stationery isn't a legal document anyway."

   Jessica is wrong because _____

   _____

   _____

4. Maria desperately needed a water pump for her car because she was stranded 200 miles from home. Joe, the mechanic, that she brought her car to realized that she was in a bind and sold her a water pump for $400. When Maria got home, her brother told her that her water pump should have cost her only $75. Maria called Joe and told him she canceled her credit card transaction with him because she was cheated. She said that she would gladly pay him $100 for the water pump. Joe said, "You can't do that, you signed the contract."

Joe is wrong because _____

_____

_____

5. A seller in California, sells ten cases of kiwi to a buyer in New Jersey. The goods are sent F.O.B. New Jersey. When the buyer received the bill for transportation charges he called the seller. The seller told him that he was responsible for the transportation charges.

Who is wrong _____ because _____

_____

_____

6. Marcia brings her television set to Milton's Electronics to be repaired. Brian, a customer, asked to see Milton's used television sets. Milton sold Marcia's set to Brian. When Marcia found out, she went to Brian's home and demanded her television set. She told Brian that he did not have the legal title to the set, and that it was hers.

Marcia is wrong because _____

_____

_____

7. A seamstress sells 1,000 dresses to a retail outlet. Since the dresses had not been made yet, they agreed to delivery in three weeks. The next week, the buyer purchases insurance on the dresses because he has already received many orders for the dresses. Two days before the dresses were to be delivered to the retail outlet, the seamstress' home caught on fire and the dresses were destroyed. The retail outlet suffered a $10,000 loss because of the fire. When the buyer filed the claim, the insurance company refused to pay, stating that the buyer had no insurable interest.

Who is wrong _____ because _____

_____

_____

Name_____ Date_____

# CHAPTER 14 - CRITICAL THINKING ACTIVITY

**Directions:** Write your own cases to show your understanding of the following concepts.

1. *Identification* _____

_____

_____

_____

_____

_____

_____

2. *Sale on approval* _____

_____

_____

_____

_____

_____

_____

_____

3. *Requirements contract* _____

_____

_____

_____

_____

_____

_____

# CHAPTER 15 - VOCABULARY ACTIVITY

**Directions:** Complete each statement by filling in the blanks with the correct term found in this chapter. Then find and circle each term in the word search that follows.

1. A warranty that the law implies through the nature of the transaction is known as a/n _____ warranty.

   ____ ____ ____ ____ ____ ____ ____

2. Goods that are reasonably fit for the ordinary purposes for which such goods are used are referred to as _____ goods.

   ____ ____ ____ ____ ____ ____ ____ ____ ____ ____ ____

3. A denial of a warranty that might otherwise exist is called a/n _____.

   ____ ____ ____ ____ ____ ____ ____ ____ ____ ____

4. A written consumer warranty that does not meet all of the requirements of a full warranty is a _____ warranty.

   ____ ____ ____ ____ ____ ____ ____

5. A statement that the seller makes as part of the contract that assures the quality, condition, or performance potential of the goods is a/n _____ warranty.

   ____ ____ ____ ____ ____ ____ ____

6. A normal seller's exaggeration about a good for sale is called _____.

   ____ ____ ____ ____ ____ ____ ____

7. An implied assurance that the seller owns and has the right to sell goods is called a warranty of _____.

   ____ ____ ____ ____ ____

8. Responsibility for damages or injury caused by a defective good is called _____ liability.

   ____ ____ ____ ____ ____ ____ ____

9. A law that allows the purchaser of an automobile to rescind the contract if the vehicle needs servicing four or more times for the same problem is called a/n _____ law.

____ ____ ____ ____ ____

10. A defense to strict liability is when the person injured by the product because he or she did r use the product the way it was intended to be used is called product _____

____ ____ ____ ____ ____ ____

```
M  E  L  E  M  O  N  S  O  D  T
E  I  I  L  M  I  S  O  V  I  C
R  M  S  H  E  E  L  O  E  S  U
C  P  A  U  R  M  P  P  U  C  D
H  L  R  P  S  S  O  O  G  L  O
A  I  X  U  R  E  E  L  A  A  R
N  E  T  F  I  L  R  E  A  I  P
T  D  Y  F  L  T  L  T  R  M  U
A  Y  M  I  L  I  M  I  T  E  D
B  O  I  N  U  T  E  C  R  S
L  T  H  G  S  I  R  H  I  S  T
E  F  N  Y  U  X  O  L  O  E  S
```

# CHAPTER 15 - FACTS AND IDEAS

**Directions:** Read each situation below to determine which warranty is being described. Place the proper name of the warranty in the blank and state your reasoning. (Use the choices shown below). If no warranty applies, place the word "none" in the blank and state your reasoning.

**Express warranty**
**Warranty of title**
**Implied warranty of merchantability**
**Implied warranty of fitness for a particular purpose**

1. Toni bought an electric drill to help build an addition to her home. After carefully reading the instructions, she started using the drill. When she started drilling, the handle broke in half and the drill injured her foot.

   A/n _____ applies because

   _____

   _____

2. Frank buys Sally's used car for $800 cash. Two months later, Trey repossesses the car from Frank. Trey sold Sally the car six months ago and she still owed $200. Sally had missed three payments on the car.

   A/n _____ applies because

   _____

   _____

3. Bonita is told by a salesperson that the computer she is purchasing will run Word Perfect and Lotus programs.

   A/n _____ applies because

   _____

   _____

4. Fran bought a pair of running shoes. On the second day of her 5-mile run, the sole came apart.

   A/n _____ applies because

   _____

   _____

5. Martha wanted to buy a roll of green wall paper that matched her dining room. The salesperson suggested a yellow instead, so she bought the yellow wall paper. When Martha got home, she realized that the yellow wall paper did not match at all.

   A/n _____ applies because

   _____

   _____

6. While Cathy was purchasing an antique chair for $1,000, the seller told Cathy, "You'd pay four times as much for that chair anywhere else." When Cathy arrived home with her new purchase, her husband, an antique dealer, told her that she would never get more than $1,500 for the chair.

   A/n _____ applies because

   _____

   _____

7. While purchasing a new motorcycle, the salesperson told Maude that the motorcycle will easily reach 80 mph. When Maude drove the motorcycle on a rural road she found it only would reach a maximum of 60 mph.

   A/n _____ applies because

   _____

   _____

8. While hanging pictures in her home, Libby could not find her hammer, so she used the handle of a pair of scissors to pound a nail in the wall. While she was pounding the nail, the scissors fell apart and cut her hand.

   A/n _____ applies because

   _____

   _____

# CHAPTER 15 - CRITICAL THINKING ACTIVITY

**Directions:** Read each advertisement below carefully to determine if the advertisement contains any express warranties or puffery. In the blanks that follow, state each ad's express warranties and/or puffery statements.

### A.

**KEEP UP WITH THE JONES**

This beautiful car will dazzle your neighbors. You will be the envy of the block with this beauty.
**$25,000**
**turbo-engine, convertible Chevy.**

### B.

*2-karat diamond ring Pear Shaped*

*Be the apple of her eye*

### C.

**\* SALE \***
**ALL ITEMS**
**50% OFF**
**CLEARANCE!**
No Refunds

### D.

HAND-MADE QUILTS

100% COTTON

GREAT NEW PRICE

LIMITED QUANTITY

WON'T LAST — HURRY

E.

**GREAT BARGAIN**

Set of wine glasses, easy care, comes with easy cleaning instruction - $20.00

F. (Create your own ad with two express warranties. List answers in blank F.)

A. _____

B. _____

C. _____

D. _____

E. _____

F. _____

# CHAPTER 16 - VOCABULARY ACTIVITY

**Directions:** Complete each sentence by filling in the blank with the proper term found in this chapter.

1. When a company must provide advertising that corrects earlier misinformation the new advertisement is called _____.

2. Misleading advertising making unjustified claims is called _____ advertising.

3. The regulation giving consumers three days to cancel a door-to-door sale is called the _____ statute.

4. When an item is advertised just to get customers in the store, and then the customer is directed to a higher-priced item, this is called _____ advertising.

5. The Act requiring an accurate description of the product on its label is called the _____ _____.

6. The Act requiring ingredients of foods to be unadulterated and to meet a specific criteria is called the _____.

7. The _____ Act helps consumers learn about the information kept by credit bureaus about them.

8. The _____ Act prevents banks from telephoning you at 2:00 a.m. about your debt.

9. The _____ Act protects consumers from unreasonable risk of injury from hazardous products.

10. The _____ Act requires sellers and lenders to disclose credit or loan terms.

# CHAPTER 16 - FACTS AND IDEAS

**Directions:** Read each statement carefully to determine why the statement is incorrect. Answer the question following each statement.

1. Margot bought an automobile. On the third day after the purchase, she decided that it used too much gasoline. When Margot tried to return the automobile back to the dealership, the sales manager told her that she signed the contract and could not return the car. Margot told the sales manager that she could return it because she had three days under the cooling-off statute.

   Margot is wrong because _____

   _____

   _____

2. Richard, a debt collector, called Amelia's employer to contact her about a debt she owed. While talking to the employer, Richard told her that Amelia owed his company $2,500. When Amelia found out that Richard had spoken to her employer about her debt, she quickly called Richard and threatened to call the Consumer Credit Commission on him. She told Richard that the Fair Credit Reporting Act protected her from his behavior.

   Amelia is wrong because _____

   _____

   _____

3. Albert read an advertisement for a new microwave priced at $150 with a 3-year warranty. When Albert arrived at the store, the salesperson tried to sell Albert another microwave priced at $250. When Albert demanded the advertised model, the salesperson told him they had none in stock, but would deliver one to him in six months. Albert told the salesperson that he was going to report him for counter advertising.

   Albert is wrong because _____

   _____

   _____

4. When Sandra realized her credit cards were missing she contacted the credit card companies. At the end of the month one of her creditors, United Card, billed her for $280 worth of merchandise she never bought. When Sandra called United Card they told her that she was responsible for the $280, since she did not notify them before the purchases were made on her card.

United Card is wrong because _____

_____

_____

5. Joanne was watching television when she saw a commercial advertisement stating that the Power Mouth Corporation apologized for the advertisement of their Minty Breath gum. The commercial stated that the gum is not 100% sugar free, as previously advertised. Joanne called her friend, Toby, and told her to turn on Channel 5 to view the bait-and-switch advertising.

Joanne is wrong because _____

_____

_____

6. The salesperson in Computer City told Jackie that the printer she was buying was the best in the market and that she would never be unhappy with this purchase. After a few days of using the printer, Jackie was very disappointed with the printer's capabilities. Jackie called Computer City to tell them that she was going to report them for false advertising.

Jackie is wrong because _____

_____

_____

# CHAPTER 16 - CRITICAL THINKING ACTIVITY

**Directions:** Read the following case and answer the questions that follow.

Daniel was having financial problems and some of his bills were not being paid. Moe's TV & Appliances called him at home at 8:00 p.m. one night to request payment on the television set that he bought two months ago. Moe's threatened to sue him if he could not pay within thirty days. Another creditor, AB Motors, called Daniel at his place of employment and spoke with one of Daniel's co-workers about his debt. AB Motors told Danny's co-worker that they would repossess his car if he did not make a payment in ten days. American Bank telephoned Daniel at 11:00 p.m. one night to try to convince Daniel to pay off his loan with them.

1. Are there any illegal practices described in this case? If so, what are they?

   _____

   _____

   _____

   _____

   _____

2. Can AB Motors legally threaten Danny with a repossession if he doesn't make a payment? Why or why not?

   _____

   _____

   _____

   _____

3. What laws did Moe's TV & Appliances violate?

   _____

   _____

   _____

   _____

4. Who should Daniel call to make a complaint about his violated rights?

_____

_____

_____

5. What could Daniel receive for these violations?

_____

_____

_____

6. What Act protects Daniel's rights from these debt collectors?

_____

_____

_____

_____

# CHAPTER 17 - VOCABULARY ACTIVITY

**Directions:** Fill in the blank spaces with the vocabulary term that best completes each sentence. Then use the letters in the boxed spaces to form the mystery term. You must unscramble the letters to form the new term.

1. A person who creates a draft is the

   ___ ☐ ___ ___ ___ ___ .

2. The person to whom a negotiable instrument is payable is the

   ___ ___ ☐ ___ ___ .

3. A draft drawn on a bank and payable to the payee on demand is called a

   ___ ___ ☐ ___ ___ .

4. A person in possession of an instrument payable to bearer or indorsed in blank is the

   ___ ___ ___ ☐ ___ ___ .

5. A signature placed on an instrument for the purpose of transferring ownership
   in the instrument is called a/n

   ___ ___ ___ ___ ___ ☐ ___ ☐ ___ ___ ___ ___ .

6. A person in possession of a negotiable instrument who is either the payee, a bearer,
   or one to whom the instrument is properly indorsed is the

   ___ ☐ ___ ___ ___ ___ .

7. Signed writings containing unconditional promises or orders to pay an exact sum
   of money, such as drafts, checks, and promissory notes are called

   ___ ☐ ___ ___ ___ ___ ___ ___ ___   ___ ___ ☐ ___ ___ .

8. A draft drawn by and payable to the seller of goods by the purchaser of the goods is a/n

   ☐ ___ ___ ___ ___   ___ ___ ___ ___ ___ ___ ___ ☐ ___ ___ .

9. Checking accounts are also called

___ ___ ___ ___ ___ ___   ___ ___ ___ ☐ ___ ☐ ___ ___.

10. The one to whom a negotiable instrument is transferred by indorsement is the

___ ___ ___ ___ ___ ☐ ___ ___.

**Key Term:** ☐ ☐ ☐ ☐ ☐ ☐ ☐ ☐ ☐ ☐
☐ ☐ ☐ ☐

**Definition:** _____

_____

_____

_____

# CHAPTER 17 - FACTS AND IDEAS

**Directions:** Read the following scenarios and answer the questions that follow.

1. Jeanie wrote a check to Robert for $35.00.  Robert brought the check to First Bank and deposited it in his checking account.

A.  Who is the drawer?_____

B.  Who is the drawee?_____

C.  Who is the payee?_____

D.  What type of indorsement would be best for Robert to use?_____


2.  Norma wrote a note promising to pay Beth $500 on January 1 of the following year for the purchase of a car.  Norma dated and signed the note and even secured the note with her automobile.

A.  What is the proper name for this paper?_____

_____

B.  Who is the maker? _____

C.  Who is the payee? _____

D.  By securing the note with her automobile, what is her automobile now referred to as?

_____


3.  Dorene Brown wrote a $100 check to her friend, Bernice Collier for a bicycle.  Bernice then indorsed the check to her daughter, Becky Collier, and gave it to her for a graduation present.

A.  What is this transfer called? _____

B.  What term describes the check now? _____

_____

C.  Who is the holder? _____

D.  What type of indorsement should Bernice use when transferring the check to Becky?

_____

# CHAPTER 17 - CRITICAL THINKING ACTIVITY

**Directions:** Write a proper indorsement for the samples below using the following guidelines.

A.  Write a blank indorsement for a check that is written to you.

B.  Write a special indorsement for a check that was written to you, but you would like to transfer it to John Sizemore.

C.  Write a qualified indorsement for a check that was written to you, but transferred to Hope Sorofman.

D.  Write a restrictive indorsement for a check that you want to make certain is deposited in your account only.

A.

B.

C.

D.

Refer to pages 399-400 in your textbook to the criteria for a negotiable instrument. Create you own scenario to write a negotiable instrument to a friend. Write the scenario in the following blanks.

_____

_____

_____

_____

_____

_____

_____

_____

_____

_____

_____

_____

_____

_____

_____

_____

# CHAPTER 18 - VOCABULARY ACTIVITY

**Directions:** Complete each sentence with the proper term found in this chapter.

1. A defense that can be used to avoid payment to all holders of a negotiable instrument is a/n _____ defense.

2. A defense that can be used to avoid payment to an ordinary holder only of a negotiable instument is a/n _____ defense.

3. An unauthorized signature of a maker or drawer is a/n _____.

4. One who takes a negotiable instrument free of all claims and most defenses of other parties is a/n _____.

5. The most common type of commercial paper are _____.

6. A check that is presented for payment more than six months after its date is a/n _____.

7. A draft drawn by a bank on itself is a/n _____.

8. A check that is guaranteed by the bank from which the individual has drawn money on his or her account is a/n _____.

9. An instrument purchased from a financial institution that can be used as cash upon a second signature by the purchaser is a/n _____.

10. When a bank agrees to extend credit to a customer if he or she writes a check for more money than exists in the account, the agreement is called a/n _____.

11. When a bank's customer instructs the bank not to pay a check, this is a/n _____.

12. When there are insufficient funds in a customer's account, and the bank pays the item and charges the customer's account, this creates a/n _____.

Name_____ Date_____

# Chapter 18 - Facts and Ideas

**Directions:** Read each situation below to determine the best type of commercial paper that should be used. (Choose from the list below.) Explain the reasons for your answer.

**Cashier's check**　　　　　　**Certified check**
**Personal check**　　　　　　**Traveler's check**

1. Cindy purchased a sweater in a local department store that does not accept cash. She does not have a personal checking account.

   She should use a/n _____

   because _____

   _____

2. Holden had to pay $3,000 in closing costs to his mortgage company for his new home. The mortgage company told him that the bank must guarantee his form of payment.

   Holden should use a/n _____

   because _____

   _____

3. Seth received his bank statement from his bank and found a $500 check that had gone through. He realized this was a check he gave to someone eight months ago. He knows his bank does not honor stale checks.

   This must have been a/n _____

   because _____

   _____

4. Gina is traveling to Europe next week. She does not like the idea of carrying around large amounts of cash.

   Gina should use _____

   because _____

   _____


5. Sharon is ready to send her utility bill in the mail. Her cousin, Rochelle, tells Sharon not to send cash in the mail.

   Sharon should use a/n _____

   because _____

   _____


6. Stephen owned a grocery store. One of his customers paid him with a type of check which required two signatures from her. The last signature, Stephen witnessed.

   This customer probably used a/n _____

   because _____

   _____


7. David issues a stop-payment order on a check.

   This must be a/n _____

   because _____

   _____

# CHAPTER 18 - CRITICAL THINKING ACTIVITY

**Directions:** Read each scenario below and answer the questions that follow.

1. Joe accepts a promissory note from Howard for $1,000 for a new computer. Then Joe negotiates the note to Celia for the purchase of a grandfather clock. Joe told Celia that the note was good and worth its value. Since Celia had known Joe for years, she accepted the instrument. Two days later, Howard found out that the computer he bought from Joe was actually a used computer. Howard refuses to pay the note.

A   Is Howard in his rights in refusing to pay the note? Why or why not?

_____

B.  What should Howard do? _____


2. Peter orders six bouquets of flowers from Heaven Scent Florist. When Peter goes to Heaven Scent to write a check for the flowers, the florist tells Peter that they do not have the bill finalized yet, but that each bouquet will cost him $30. Peter gave the check to the florist leaving the dollar amount blank. When Peter's monthly bank statement arrived, he noticed a canceled check to Heaven Scent Florist for $350.

A.  Can Peter hold the bank responsible for the $170 difference? Why or why not?

_____

B.  What can Peter do to recover his $170? _____

_____

C.  How should Peter have settled the payment originally? _____

_____

3.  Create your own scenario and questions in the following blanks describing a case involving a stop-payment order.

_____

_____

_____

_____

_____

_____

_____

_____

_____

_____

_____

_____

_____

_____

_____

_____

_____

Name_____ Date_____

# CHAPTER 19 - VOCABULARY ACTIVITY

**Directions:** Choose *ten* of the following terms from the list below. Define and give an example of each term you choose.

artisan's lien
creditor's composition agreement
foreclosure
guaranty
innkeeper's lien
secured creditor
unsecured creditor

bankruptcy
garnishment
homestead exemption
mechanic's lien
suretyship
writ of execution

1. Term: _____

   Definition: _____

   _____

   Example: _____

   _____


2. Term: _____

   Definition: _____

   _____

   Example: _____

   _____


3. Term: _____

   Definition: _____

   _____

   Example: _____

   _____

4. Term: _____

   Definition: _____

   _____

   Example: _____

   _____


5. Term: _____

   Definition: _____

   _____

   Example: _____

   _____


6. Term: _____

   Definition: _____

   _____

   Example: _____

   _____


7. Term: _____

   Definition: _____

   _____

   Example: _____

   _____

8. Term: _____

   Definition: _____

   _____

   Example: _____

   _____


9. Term: _____

   Definition: _____

   _____

   Example: _____

   _____


10. Term: _____

    Definition: _____

    _____

    Example: _____

    _____

Name_____ Date_____

# CHAPTER 19 - FACTS AND IDEAS

**Directions:** Read the following situations and answer the questions that follow.

1. Pedro purchases a tractor for $24,500. He takes out a loan from American Bank for $20,000 and pays a down payment of $4,500. Pedro agrees to a lien on the tractor if he does not pay the debt.

A. Who is the creditor?_____

B. Who is the debtor?_____

C. What rights does the creditor have against Pedro if he defaults on the loan?

_____

_____


2. Joshua brings his computer to Computer Center for repairs. Two months go by and Joshua does not come in to pay for the repairs or to pick up the computer.

A. Can Computer Center keep Joshua's computer until he pays for the repairs?
   Why or why not?_____

_____

B. If two more months go by and Joshua still does not come in to pay for the computer, what rights does Computer Center have?_____

_____

C. What rights does Joshua have if Computer Center sells his computer?

_____

_____

3. Bill owes Furniture City $800 for a dining room set he purchased a year ago. Furniture City received a court-ordered right to seize $50 from every pay check Bill receives from his employer.

A. What is this court order called?_____

_____

B. How much of Bill's paycheck can Furniture City legally receive? _____

_____

C. Who was this court order served to? _____

_____

D. Can Bill's employer fire him because of this event? Why or why not?

_____

_____


4. Troy owes Linda $15,000. Linda takes Troy to court and is awarded a judgment against Troy for $15,000. Troy's home is worth $35,000, but he has a homestead exemption of $20,000. Troy decides to sell his home to satisfy the judgment. He sells it for $32,000.

A. How much will Linda receive from the sale of the home?_____

B. How much will Troy receive from the sale of his home?_____

C. How can Linda get the remainder of the debt owed to her?

_____

_____

115

# CHAPTER 19 - CRITICAL THINKING ACTIVITY

**Directions:** Read the following case and discuss the questions that follow to determine which type of bankruptcy would be best for Helena.

Helena decided to claim a voluntary bankruptcy because she simply could not afford to make all of her payments. Helena is single. She is a banker who makes $20,000 a year. She rents an apartment in which she pays $500 per month. She owns two automobiles, one is fully paid for, the other she still owes $5,500 on. She has three credit cards with a total outstanding debt of $40,000.

1. Can Helena file Chapter 7 Bankruptcy?_____

   If so, what will be the probable results? _____

   _____

   _____

   _____

2. Can Helena file Chapter 11 Bankruptcy?_____

   If so, what will be the probable results?_____

   _____

   _____

   _____

   _____

3. Can Helena file Chapter 12 Bankruptcy?_____

   If so, what will be the probable results?_____

   _____

   _____

   _____

4. Can Helena file Chapter 13 Bankruptcy?_____

   If so, what will be the probable results?_____

   _____

   _____

   _____


5. Which Chapter of Bankruptcy do you think Helena should file and why?

   _____

   _____

   _____

   _____


6. What are the disadvantages of claiming bankruptcy?

   _____

   _____

   _____

   _____

# CHAPTER 20 - VOCABULARY ACTIVITY

**Directions:** Fill in the blank spaces with the vocabulary term from this chapter that best completes each sentence. Then write the numbered letters in the appropriate blanks to solve the mystery term.

1. A person authorized by another to represent or act for him or her is a/n _____.

   ___ ___ ___ ___ ___
        1

2. A person who works for another is a/n _____.

   ___ ___ ___ ___ ___ ___ ___ ___
        2

3. A person who authorizes another to act on his or her behalf is a/n _____.

   ___ ___ ___ ___ ___ ___ ___ ___ ___
      3

4. Accepting and allowing an obligation to be legal that you could have avoided is called _____.

   ___ ___ ___ ___ ___ ___ ___ ___ - ___ ___ ___ ___
                                        8

5. A person who is hired to perform a particular task and has all or most control over their own performance is a/n _____.

   ___ ___ ___ ___ ___ ___ ___ ___ ___ ___ ___
                                    6

   ___ ___ ___ - ___ ___ ___ ___ ___ ___ ___
             11

6. A _____ principal is one in which the third party knows who the principal is in a transaction.

   ___ ___ ___ ___ ___ ___ ___ ___ ___
    5

7. A formal document authorizing another to act as one's agent is a _____.

___ ___ ___ ___ ___   ___ ___

___ ___ ___ ___ ___ ___ ___ ___
         7

8. The relationship involving trust between the agent and the principal is called a _____ relationship.

___ ___ ___ ___ ___ ___ ___ ___ ___
         10

9. A notice given to the general public usually by a publication of an advertisement in a newspaper is called a _____ notice.

___ ___ ___ ___ ___ ___ ___ ___ ___ ___ ___ ___
      4

10. A principal whose identity and existence are unknown by a third party is a/n _____ principal.

___ ___ ___ ___ ___ ___ ___ ___ ___ ___ ___
         9

**Key Term:** ___ ___ ___ ___ ___ ___ ___ ___ ___ ___
              3   1   4   2   7   8   5   1   11  6

              ___ ___ ___ ___ ___ ___ ___ ___
               4   10   2   1   3   9   7   3

**Definition:** _____

_____

_____

_____

_____

# CHAPTER 20 - FACTS AND IDEAS

**Directions:** Identify the incorrect term in each of the following statements. Then rewrite the sentence correctly in the blank that follows.

1. Pierre hired Sondra to work as a cashier in his grocery store. This makes Sondra a principal.

   _____

   _____

   _____

   _____

2. Jeanine wanted to hire an agent to evaluate her office for six weeks and give professional suggestions on how her office can be run more efficiently.

   _____

   _____

   _____

   _____

3. Debra was visiting her friend, Norma, in her clothing store. While Debra was busy with a customer, Norma convinced another customer to buy a gown. Debra thanked Norma for helping her out. Norma became an agent by estoppel.

   _____

   _____

   _____

   _____

4. One of the duties an agent owes a principal is compensation.

_____

_____

_____

_____

5. One of the principal's duties to an agent is to keep accurate records of all property or money distributed.

_____

_____

_____

_____

6. Frederick gave a power of attorney to his brother, Carl, in case that he was incapacitated in the hospital. Frederick wants Carl to be the one to make any decisions about his health care if he can not.

_____

_____

_____

_____

7. Michael bought an acre of land from Zeke. Michael thought he was buying the land from Zeke, but Zeke was actually acting as an agent for Carlos. Carlos w as a disclosed principal.

_____

_____

_____

_____

8. Savannah was injured while taking horseback riding lessons from Tiffany. Savannah decided to sue the owner of the stables instead of Tiffany because of the fudiciary theory.

_____

_____

_____

_____

9. An agency relationship was terminated by act of the parties when the principal went bankrupt.

_____

_____

_____

_____

10. The law allows the principal to protect himself or herself from liability to unknown third parties by giving all parties respondent superior.

_____

_____

_____

_____

Name_____ Date_____

# CHAPTER 20 - CRITICAL THINKING ACTIVITY

**Directions:** Design and write your own Legal Focus Problem or Legal Focus Example describing a situation involving each of the following concepts.

1. A principal-independent contractor relationship

_____

_____

_____

_____

_____

_____

_____

_____

2. A power of attorney

_____

_____

_____

_____

_____

_____

_____

_____

3. A termination of an agency by act of the parties

_____

_____

_____

_____

_____

_____

_____

_____

# CHAPTER 21 - VOCABULARY ACTIVITY

**Directions:** Match the term with the proper definition by placing the correct letter in the blank.

_____ 1. the right given to a union to bargain with the employer over terms of employment

_____ 2. a company where employees are required to join a union after a short time on the job

_____ 3. a requirement that an employer have a legitimate provable reason to fire an employee

_____ 4. an order by a court not to do something

_____ 5. a company where employees must belong to a union before being hired

_____ 6. an employee who tells the public about illegal activities in his or her organization

_____ 7. a refusal by a group of workers to work for their employer

_____ 8. pressuring one company not to continue to do business with a second company, who is the employer

_____ 9. a state law that makes it illegal for union membership to be required for continued employment in any business

_____ 10. when an employer agrees not to do business with other employers who do not use union workers

A. strike

B. injunction

C. secondary boycott

D. hot-cargo contracts

E. closed shop

F. collective bargaining

G. just cause

H. right-to-work law

I. union shop

J. whistleblower

11. Define the term "polygraph" _____

_____

_____

# CHAPTER 21 - FACTS AND IDEAS

**Directions:** Answer the following questions with short answers. Use the blanks that follow the question.

1. Why was the Taft-Hartley Act passed?

   _____

   _____

   _____

2. What type of shop was made illegal in all states by the Taft-Hartley Act? Describe this shop

   _____

   _____

   _____

3. What two groups of people cannot legally hold a union office?

   _____

   _____

   _____

4. Discuss some of the changes that have taken place in United States employment contracts since the just-cause provision.

   _____

   _____

   _____

5. Name an employment situation in which drug testing is permitted

   _____

   _____

   _____

6. What are some ways employers monitor employee performances?

_____

_____

_____

7. What is the difference between hot-cargo contracts and secondary boycotts?

_____

_____

_____

8. What are the similarities between hot-cargo contracts and secondary boycotts?

_____

_____

_____

# CHAPTER 21 - CRITICAL THINKING ACTIVITY

**Directions:** The following story contains activities between an employer and a union. Read the activities of each and answer the questions that follow.

United Metal Industries (UMI) is a manufacturing company that produces widgets. The union is considering a strike because management did not agree to all of the unions' demands during collective bargaining. The union of UMI consists of 25% of all the personnel employed at UMI. Following are some of the reasons that the employer and the union are having problems:

Last year management laid off thirty employees out of necessity. Twenty-five of the employees laid-off were union members. To protect the union members, the union voted to require all new employees hired to be a union member before being hired. To ease the contention between the union and the company, management decided to contribute $10,000 to the union. In hopes to persuade the management to change their minds on some of the negotiation issues, the union persuaded TMS, a customer of UMI, to not do any business with UMI until negotiations were finalized.

1. Which union activities are illegal or unfair? Why?

_____

_____

_____

_____

_____

_____

2. Which employer activities are illegal or unfair? Why?

_____

_____

_____

_____

_____

_____

3. What actions do you think the union should have taken to get what they wanted?

_____

_____

_____

_____

_____

_____

4. What actions do you think the employer should have taken to get what they wanted?

_____

_____

_____

_____

_____

_____

# CHAPTER 22 - VOCABULARY ACTIVITY

**Directions:** Complete each sentence with the correct term found in this chapter. Then place the numbered letters in the corresponding blanks that follow to solve the mystery term.

1. Intentional discrimination against a certain group of persons is called _____ discrimination.

   ___ ___ ___ ___ ___ ___ ___ ___ ___ -
           2

   ___ ___ ___ ___ ___ ___ ___ ___ ___

2. A program that gives qualified minorities and women preferential treatment when employees are hired and promoted is called _____  _____.

   ___ ___ ___ ___ ___ ___ ___ ___ ___ ___
            8

   ___ ___ ___ ___ ___ ___
   1

3. A group of persons specifically protected by the Civil Rights Act of 1964 from discrimination is called a/n _____.

   ___ ___ ___ ___ ___ ___ ___ ___ ___   ___ ___ ___ ___ ___
            3

4. Worker's compensation is a form of _____ insurance.

   ___ ___ - ___ ___ ___ ___ ___
       4

5. _____ is a health insurance program that provides health benefits for disabled persons or persons over 65 years of age.

   ___ ___ ___ ___ ___ ___ ___ ___
    5

133

6. Giving an employee legal ownership of his or her pension funds before reaching retirement age is called _____.

___ ___ ___ ___ ___ ___ ___
      6

7. The act that requires businesses be maintained free from safety and health hazards is the _____ Act.

___ ___ ___ ___ ___ ___ ___ ___ ___ ___ ___
                  7

___ ___ ___ ___ ___ ___    ___ ___ ___

___ ___ ___ ___ ___ ___

**Mystery Term:** ___ ___ ___ ___ ___    ___ ___ ___ ___ ___
         2   8   7   5   1     4   1   3   7   6

**Definition:** _____

_____

_____

_____

_____

# CHAPTER 22 - FACTS AND IDEAS

**Directions:** Read each scenario to determine what Act from this chapter covers the individual. Write the Act that covers them in the blank that follows.

1. Lorene was fired from her warehouse manager position because she became pregnant and unable to perform all of her duties on the job.

   _____

2. Paul, 52, was an assembly line worker for a major automobile manufacturer. He has worked for the company for eighteen years. His supervisor just told him that he would have to retire next year or be laid-off.

   _____

3. Sophie, a secretary, tripped and broke her arm while carrying a heavy box from one office to another.

   _____

4. Ann was the only woman of four Training Managers of a bank. She received a $5,000 bonus at the end of the year, but learned that the other three Training Managers (all men) received a $7,500 bonus. Ann knew the bonus was not a performance bonus, but an appreciation bonus. Ann had been working for the bank longer than two of the other men.

   _____

5. Harvey, a physics teacher for a public high school, was fired from his position when his employer learned that he had AIDS.

   _____

6. Emilio, 60, was laid off from his $18.00 per hour Waste Management job. The company never called him back for his original position, but offered him a janitorial position at $9.00 per hour. Emilio had worked for this company for ten years. He learned later that they hired a 28-year old to take his old position for $12.00 per hour.

   _____

7. Maria applied for a server position at La Normandie, an exclusive French Restaurant. The manager told her that they do not hire female servers.

_____

8. Peter was a solderer at Teco Manufacturing. One day Peter's supervisor asked him to solder a piece of equipment. When Peter told his supervisor that he left his safety glasses in his locker, his supervisor told him not to worry about it, and instructed him to solder.

_____

9. Belinda was in a bad car accident and was left paralyzed. She could no longer work.

_____

10. Bill had worked for General Contractors for 22 years, but when he submitted his notice for retirement, his supervisor told him that his pension would not kick in until he worked there eight more years.

_____

# CHAPTER 22 - CRITICAL THINKING ACTIVITY

**Directions:** Read each case to determine if the person involved had their legal rights violated. if so, state what laws protect them. If not, write "NO" in the blank and explain why not.

1. Carmen, an African American, just received her bachelor's degree in engineering. She interviewed with ABC Company for an engineering position, which she was highly qualified for. After the interview, the interviewer called her and told her that she was just not the type of person that they were looking for. The next week, she saw the advertisement for that position in the newspaper again. After a little research, Carmen learned that the company employed only one black person of a staff of 280.

   Were Carmen's rights violated? If so, which ones? _____

   _____

2. Morton was a part-time proofreader for General Publishing Company. While driving to work one morning, Morton was involved in an automobile accident. He was injured and hospitalized for three weeks. When he called his employer for worker's compensation papers, his employer said that he could not claim anything under Worker's Compensation for this incident.

   Were Morton's rights violated? If so, which ones? _____

   _____

3. Nelson, a white male, interviewed for a computer analyst position with a major corporation in the local area. The interviewer told him that he was more highly qualified than any other candidate he had interviewed yet. When the interviewer called Nelson two days later, Nelson was told that they had to give the job to someone else. When Nelson asked why, the interviewer told him because of affirmative action reasons.

   A. Were Nelson's rights violated? If so, which ones? _____

   _____

   B. What did the interviewer mean by "affirmative action"? _____

   _____

   _____

# CHAPTER 23 - VOCABULARY ACTIVITY

**Directions:** Fill in the blanks with the correct vocabulary term found in this chapter.

1. An accounting term for cash or other personal property is
   a/n _____.

2. An accounting term for money or other assets that are invested in the business
   is called _____.

3. A business owned by one person, and is the easiest form of business to enter into
   is the _____  _____.

4. A written agreement between partners in a business stating each partner's rights
   and duties to the partnership is called a/n _____
   of _____.

5. When a business owner's personal assets, as well as business assets, are at risk in the
   running of the business, this is called _____ liability.

6. An accounting term for the value of the business that exceeds its asset value is

   _____.

7. Each partner has an equal right to use partnership property for business purposes; they
   are all co-owners of specific partnership property. This form of ownership is called
   _____ in _____.

8. Sharing responsibility for debts and obligations in a partnership is called

   _____  _____.

9. When one partner has complete and separate responsibility for an entire obligation,
   it is called _____  _____.

10. When one or more partner indicates an intention to quit the partnership, the term used for the end of the partnership is called _____.

11. A partnership in which there are general partners and there are partners whose liability is only equal to their investment is called a/n _____ partnership.

12. When two or more persons or businesses combine their interests in a one-time business effort, this is called a _____.

# CHAPTER 23 - FACTS AND IDEAS

**Directions:** Read the Legal Perspective section found on Pages 563-566 in your textbook before beginning this assignment. Then read each scenario to determine which form of business is being described. The choices of business ownership forms are:

**sole proprietorship**

**general partnership**

**limited partnership**

**corporation**

**franchise**

1. Tracy owns and runs a small florist shop in which she employs two sales clerks. The other owner, Dill, invested 50% of the initial investment to start up the business, but has few rights to make management decisions. Tracy earns 80% of the profits.

   This form of business is a _____

2. Daphne owns a small donut shop in which she makes all of the decisions. She makes all the profits and suffers all the losses by herself. She employs five servers.

   This form of business is a _____

3. Margaret operates a small restaurant by herself. She has hired ten employees to help her. Once a week she must order supplies from the seller of the business.

   This form of business is a _____

4. Lenny and Tony own an Italian restaurant. They both manage the restaurant and both share the profits and losses equally.

   This form of business is a _____

5. Rico owns and operates a music store. He enjoys this business because he is musically inclined and he would not lose any of his personal assets if the business failed. However, the start up costs for this particular business was higher than any of the other forms of business. Sometimes his business profits are taxed twice.

   This form of business is a _____

6. Dave and Jeanette decide to open a surf board retail business together. They formed and signed a partnership agreement that stated Dave would handle the sales and Jeanette would handle the accounting procedures. They would split the profits equally every month.

   This form of business is a _____

# CHAPTER 23 - CRITICAL THINKING ACTIVITY

**Directions:** Read the story below and answer the questions that follow. Ronda needs your help in deciding which form of business she should enter into. Explain your reasoning.

Ronda has worked for a computer dating service for three years. Since she knows a lot about the business, she decides to open her own computer dating service. She is not sure what form of business that she should enter into. She has her own computer at home which she can use for the business if she purchases her own software, modem, and phone line. Ronda has $10,000 in her savings account to help her get started. Ronda's friend, Amy, has $15,000 that she offered to Ronda as an investment in the business if Ronda allowed her to help her run the business and be a part of it. Ronda is considering Amy's offer; however, Amy has no experience in computer dating. Amy has five years experience in sales.

1. Ronda should/should not consider entering into a sole proprietorship because ·

_____

_____

_____

_____

2. Ronda should/should not consider entering into a general partnership because

_____

_____

_____

_____

3. Ronda should/should not consider entering into a limited partnership because

_____

_____

_____

_____

4. Ronda should/should not consider entering into a joint venture because

_____

_____

_____

_____

5. I think Ronda's best choice of business ownership would be the

_____

because _____

_____

_____

_____

# CHAPTER 24 - VOCABULARY ACTIVITY

**Directions:** Complete each sentence by filling in the blank with the proper word from the chapter. Then find and circle the word in the word search that follows.

1. An ownership interest in a corporation measured in units of shares is called

   _____.

2. A legal entity created by law which is a form of business ownership is called
   a/n _____.

3. A corporation that was formed in another country, but does business in the U.S.
   is a/n _____ corporation.

4. A corporation created and run only in its original home state is a/n
   _____ corporation.

5. A corporation owned by a few persons for private benefit is a/n
   _____ corporation.

6. A corporation formed that pays no income taxes because it earns no profit is a/n
   _____ corporation.

7. A person who takes the preliminary steps in organizing a corporation is called
   the _____.

8. Agreements made before the corporation is formed are called
   _____ contracts.

9. The document describing the corporation which is made by the incorporators and sent
   to a state official is called the _____ of incorporation.

10. The state issues a certificate of incorporation, which is also known as the corporate

    _____.

11. A distribution of corporate profits to a shareholder is called a/n _____.

12. The usual stock which allows stockholders a voting right is called
_____ stock.

13. The legal combination of two or more corporations so that only one of the two corporations continue to exist is called a _____.

14. The legal death of a corporation is called a/n _____.

```
P   C   O   R   P   O   R   A   T   I   O   N
N   O   N   P   R   O   F   I   T   E   A   A
L   E   T   T   E   S   D   O   L   R   I   R
P   I   T   N   I   L   O   S   V   E   R   T
R   O   A   V   N   U   M   R   R   T   E   I
I   N   I   O   C   O   E   T   E   R   I   C
V   D   O   L   O   G   S   E   T   A   A   L
A   L   N   O   R   S   T   H   O   H   K   E
T   R   O   E   P   R   I   R   M   C   M   S
E   O   M   E   O   C   C   I   O   O   C   L
P   I   M   T   R   H   E   T   R   I   S   E
S   T   O   S   A   E   S   B   P   E   R   A
M   I   C   C   T   T   I   H   T   S   H   L
E   B   E   D   I   V   I   D   E   N   D   I
D   I   S   S   O   L   U   T   I   O   N   E
S   T   I   N   N   A   N   M   T   H   E   N
```

# CHAPTER 24 - FACTS AND IDEAS

**Directions:** Write questions that would correspond to the answers listed below.

1. Question: _____

   _____

   Answer: Any company listed on the New York Stock Exchange is this form
   of corporation.

2. Question: _____

   _____

   Answer: Sometimes a corporation pays taxes twice, once on the profit and once again
   on the profit if it is given as dividends to the stockholders.

3. Question: _____

   _____

   Answer: XYZ Corporation does business in Georgia, Florida, and South Carolina, but
   was incorporated in Delaware.

4. Question: _____

   _____

   Answer: A corporation whose shares are held by members of a family or by a
   few persons.

5. Question: _____

   _____

   Answer: This includes the corporate name, the nature and purpose, duration, capital
   structure, and internal organization of the proposed business.

6. Question: _____

   _____

   Answer: If the state approves it, then it issues a certificate of incorporation, the
   corporate charter.

7. Question: _____
   _____

   Answer:  You could send a proxy to represent yourself.

8. Question: _____
   _____

   Answer:  They are elected into office.

9. Question: _____
   _____

   Answer:  He or she should make a full disclosure of that interest and not vote on
   the transaction.

10. Question: _____
    _____

    Answer:  They are paid their dividends first and  their investment  back first upon the
    dissolution of the corporation.

11. Question: _____
    _____

    Answer:  A right given to a shareholder to purchase a proportional amount of stock
    when it is issued.

12. Question: _____
    _____

    Answer:  When two corporations legally continue to form a new corporation.

# CHAPTER 24 - CRITICAL THINKING ACTIVITY

**Directions:** Read the following case and answer the questions that follow.

In 1990, Mark and Millie Rosenberg started a business. They both shared management duties, profits, and losses equally. By 1992, their business prospered so much that they decided to expand and turn it into a corporation. However, the Rosenbergs wanted to keep the corporation's shares limited to family members only. In 1992, they did incorporate; keeping all of the shares in the family. Their business continued to grow unexpectedly, so in 1994 they had plans to expand their business even more. However, they needed $200,000 to do so. The only way they could do this is to make their stock available for purchase to the general public. So they did. They sold 50,000 shares of stock for $4.00 per share in the New York Stock Exchange. Twenty-five percent of their stock was preferred 5% and the remainder was common stock.

1. What type of business ownership did Mark and Millie have when they started their business?

_____

2. In 1992, what type of corporation did they begin?

_____

3. In 1994, what type of corporation did they turn their business into?

_____

4. In 1994, Marie owns 200 shares of stock in the Rosenberg corporation. She received the same amount of dividends every quarter, but could not vote in any of the stockholder's meeting. Which type of stock does she own?

_____

5. Samuel owns 100 shares of common stock in the Rosenberg corporation. How many votes is he allowed during a stockholder's meeting?

_____

6. If Samuel in Question #5 sold his stocks at $4.50 per share, how much money would he receive?

_____

7. If Marie in Question #4 sold her stocks at $3.75 per share, how much profit would she receive from the sale?

_____

8. Suppose the Rosenberg corporation decided to distribute dividends of $30,000 to their stockholders. How much would the preferred stockholders receive if the face value of the stock was $10.00 per share?

_____

# CHAPTER 25 - VOCABULARY ACTIVITY

**Directions:** Fill in the blanks with the appropriate terms from this chapter.

1. Federal agencies that are a sub-branch of the executive branch of government set up to carry out laws are called _____

___ ___ ___ ___ ___ ___ ___ ___ ___ ___ ___ ___ ___

___ ___ ___ ___ ___ ___ ___ ___
    1

2. _____ consists of rules, regulations, orders, and decisions of administrative agencies.

___ ___ ___ ___ ___ ___ ___ ___ ___ ___ ___ ___ ___ ___
                                               5

___ ___ ___

3. The first true independent regulatory agency was the _____.

___ ___ ___ ___ ___ ___ ___ ___ ___ ___
  4

___ ___ ___ ___ ___ ___ ___ ___
    6

___ ___ ___ ___ ___ ___ ___ ___ ___ ___

4. When Congress passes legislation establishing an agency and broadly defining its powers, it is called _____.

___ ___ ___ ___ ___ ___ ___ ___

___ ___ ___ ___ ___ ___ ___ ___ ___ ___ ___

5. The four functions of the administrative agencies is called the _____.

___ ___ ___ ___ ___ ___ ___ ___ ___ ___ ___ ___ ___ ___
  2

___ ___ ___ ___ ___ ___ ___

6. An order to produce a witness or a thing is called a/n _____.

   ___ ___ ___ ___ ___ ___ ___ ___
        7

7. The official publication of the federal government for all agency regulations
   is the _____.

   ___ ___ ___ ___ ___ ___ ___ ___   ___ ___ ___ ___ ___ ___ ___ ___

8. A government employee appointed to hear and decide administrative agency hearings
   is called a/n _____.

   ___ ___ ___ ___ ___ ___ ___ ___ ___ ___ ___ ___ ___ ___

   ___ ___ ___   ___ ___ ___ ___ ___
           3

9. The trial-like proceedings that take place before an ALJ are called _____.

   ___ ___ ___ ___ ___ ___ ___ ___ ___ ___ ___ ___ ___ ___

   ___ ___ ___ ___ ___ ___ ___ ___
                   9

10. The challenger in an administrative agency suit must have a direct stake in the outcome
    of the judicial proceeding.  This is called _____.

    ___ ___ ___ ___ ___ ___ ___ ___   ___ ___   ___ ___ ___
                                8

**New Term**:  ___ ___ ___ ___ ___ ___ ___ ___ ___ ___ ___ ___
              1   2   3   7   2   4   6   1   5   4   8   9

**Definition**:  _____

_____

_____

_____

# CHAPTER 25 - FACTS AND IDEAS

**Directions:** Answer the following questions with short statements. You may find these questions to be helpful in studying for the chapter test.

1. What is the role of the President in independent regulatory agencies?

_____

_____

_____

2. Why was the first independent regulatory agency (the ICC) created?

_____

_____

_____

3. Why did FDR establish regulatory programs?

_____

_____

_____

4. What are the four basic legally related functions that most administrative agencies serve?

_____

_____

_____

5. What are the two most important investigative tools available to administrative agencies?

_____

_____

_____

6. What are the three types of rules that an agency may create?

_____

_____

_____

7. What is the process of adjudication?

_____

_____

_____

8. Describe what takes place at an administrative hearing.

_____

_____

_____

9. What is de novo?

_____

_____

_____

10. Why are courts reluctant to interfere with regulatory agencies?

_____

_____

_____

# CHAPTER 25 - CRITICAL THINKING ACTIVITY

**Directions:** Read the Legal Perspective about Environmental Law found on pages 610-613 in your textbook. Take a few minutes to think about some of the environmental hazards or humanitarian problems that your local area is experiencing. Make up two new regulatory agencies that you think would help today's society. Write a proposal for the agencies by writing (a) the name of the agency (b) what the agency regulates, and (c) why we need it.

1. _____

_____

_____

_____

_____

_____

_____

_____

2. _____

_____

_____

_____

_____

_____

_____

_____

# CHAPTER 26 - VOCABULARY ACTIVITY

**Directions:** Fill in the blanks with the proper term found in this chapter.  Then unscramble the boxed letters to discover the mystery term.

1. The legal age of adulthood is called _____.

   ___ ⬜ ___ ___ ___ ___ ___ ___

2. When a minor becomes free of parental control and custody, the minor is

   _____.

   ___ ___ ___ ___ ___ ___ ⬜ ___ ___ ___ ___

3. Any individual under the legal age of majority is called a/n _____.

   ___ ___ ___ ___ ⬜

4. If a minor student does not attend school during the legally required ages of his or her state, the minor is considered _____.

   ___ ___ ___ ___ ⬜ ___

5. The state law that specifies the ages between which a minor must attend a public or private school is the _____ _____ law.

   ___ ___ ___ ___ ___ ___ ___ ___ ___ ___

   ___ ___ ___ ___ ___ ___ ___ ___ ___ ⬜ ___

6. When a student is suspended from school for a long time or kicked out of school completely, this is called _____.

   ___ ___ ___ ___ ___ ⬜ ___ ___ ___

7. The use of physical pain to punish a student is called _____.

   ___ ___ ___ ___ ___ ___ ___ ___

   ⬜ ___ ___ ___ ___ ___ ___ ___ ___ ___

8. Contracts that can be canceled by one party, but not the other is a/n
_____ contract.

\_\_\_ \_\_\_ \_\_\_ \_\_\_ ☐ \_\_\_ \_\_\_ \_\_\_

9. The doctrine which made children unable to sue their parents for personal injuries was called _____ _____.

\_\_\_ \_\_\_ \_\_\_ \_\_\_ \_\_\_ \_\_\_

\_\_\_ \_\_\_ \_\_\_ \_\_\_ \_\_\_ \_\_\_ ☐ \_\_\_

10. A minor who has committed an act that is a crime for adults is considered a/n _____.

\_\_\_ \_\_\_ \_\_\_ ☐ \_\_\_ \_\_\_ \_\_\_ \_\_\_ \_\_\_

11. A sentence of confinement for a fixed period of time, specified by law is a/n _____ _____.

\_\_\_ \_\_\_ \_\_\_ \_\_\_ ☐ \_\_\_ \_\_\_ \_\_\_ \_\_\_ \_\_\_ \_\_\_

\_\_\_ \_\_\_ \_\_\_ \_\_\_ \_\_\_ \_\_\_ \_\_\_

12. Juveniles who engage in forbidden acts for minors, but not crimes, are called _____ _____.

\_\_\_ \_\_\_ ☐ \_\_\_ \_\_\_ \_\_\_

\_\_\_ \_\_\_ \_\_\_ \_\_\_ \_\_\_ ☐ \_\_\_ \_\_\_

**Mystery Term:** ☐ ☐ ☐ ☐ ☐
☐ ☐ ☐ ☐ ☐ ☐

**Definition:** _____

_____

_____

_____

_____

158

# CHAPTER 26 - FACTS AND IDEAS

**Directions:** Read each situation below and write in the blanks that follow an explanation of why the person in question is wrong in their thinking.

1. Polly, 16, wanted to move out of her parents' home and be on her own. Her parents refused to agree to this arrangement. Polly has a part time job making $5.00 hour working 15 hours per week. She told her parents that once she saved up $500, she would move out because if a minor has a job they automatically become emancipated.

   Polly is wrong because _____

   _____

   _____

   _____

   _____

2. Denise and Frederica live in Little Rock, Arkansas. Denise told Frederica that she was going to drop out of school when she was 17 years old. Frederica told her that the law states that she can drop out at 16.

   Frederica is wrong because _____

   _____

   _____

   _____

   _____

3. Timothy was sent to the vice-principal of his high school for throwing a paper airplane in class. The vice-principal told Timothy that he was suspended for one month for disrupting the class. Timothy told the vice-principal that this was unfair. The vice-principal said, "No it is not, what is unfair is your disrupting the classroom."

The vice-principal is wrong because _____

_____

_____

_____

_____

4. Janice was told to attend a disciplinary hearing because she was accused of drawing graffiti on the school's walls. Attending the hearing was Janice, two teachers, and the principal. The principal told her that he had proof it was her who drew the graffiti, and was therefore suspended for two weeks. Janice stood and told them that this was unfair. The principal replied, "You had a hearing."

The principal is wrong because _____

_____

_____

_____

_____

5. The principal of Hilltop High School ordered a search in all of the student's lockers because there had been an increase in drug abuse in the state. One student, Lora, was standing at her locker when the search began. Lora yelled, "this is an invasion of our privacy." The administrator conducting the search replied, "We have a right to search these lockers any time we want — we own them."

The administrator is wrong because _____

_____

_____

_____

_____

160

# CHAPTER 26 - CRITICAL THINKING ACTIVITY

**Directions:** Read the case problems below and answer the questions that follow.

1. Nathan, 17, bought a used automobile from Sam's Used Cars. Sam knew Nathan was a minor, but he figured it was a ten-year old car worth only $300 and he got $500 from Nathan for it. Two weeks later, Nathan had three friends in his car and was driving recklessly when he hit a stranded motor home on the side of the road.

   A. Can Nathan still return the car to Sam's Used Cars?

   _____

   _____

   _____

   _____

   B. Is Nathan liable for the motor home's damages or are his parent's liable?

   _____

   _____

   _____

   _____

   C. Change the situation so that Nathan's parents would be liable. Write the different version below.

   _____

   _____

   _____

   _____

   _____

   _____

   _____

   _____

2. Jolene, 16, was arrested for robbing a video store. The arresting police officer just happened to see Jolene run a red light, so he pulled her over and searched her car. In her glove compartment, he found a pistol and $2,500 in cash. The officer took Jolene in for questioning, but Jolene denied committing any crime. When Jolene asked to be released, the officer told her that she could not have bail. The officer told her he might release her to her parents.

A. Did the police officer have a right to pull Jolene over? Why or why not?

_____

_____

_____

_____

B. Did the police officer have a right to search Jolene's car? Why or why not?

_____

_____

_____

_____

C. Will the gun and the money found in Jolene's car be evidence against her?

_____

_____

_____

_____

D. Was the police officer within his rights when he refused to grant Jolene bail? Why or why not?

_____

_____

_____

_____

# CHAPTER 27 - VOCABULARY ACTIVITY

**Directions:** Fill in the blank with the proper term found in this chapter. Then find and circle the term in the word puzzle that follows.

1. The legal union of a husband and wife is called a/n _____.

2. Property acquired and owned by both husband and wife jointly during the marriage is _____ property.

3. Property individually owned by one spouse is called _____ property.

4. An informal marriage occurring when persons agree to be and act like they are married, but have no marriage license is a/n _____ _____ marriage.

5. When separate property is mixed with community property, _____ occurs.

6. A legal process that creates a parent-child relationship is called _____.

7. The termination of a marriage because some defect existed when the marriage was begun is a/n _____.

8. The modern term for the termination of a marriage by court order is called a/n _____.

9. A regular payment made by one spouse to the other spouse for living expenses is called _____.

10. When a child is taken away from his or her parents and put in someone else's home temporarily, this is called _____ _____.

```
M  S  E  P  A  R  A  T  E
I  T  E  I  S  A  W  O  N
A  C  H  L  C  N  R  E  D
N  H  C  F  O  O  V  F  L
N  U  O  A  M  I  L  O  D
U  S  M  N  M  T  O  S  N
L  B  M  D  I  P  U  T  O
M  Y  O  R  N  O  R  E  I
E  N  N  L  G  D  G  R  T
N  O  L  E  L  A  W  C  U
T  M  A  S  I  T  I  A  L
T  I  W  R  N  S  I  R  O
H  L  R  E  G  Y  Y  E  S
I  A  S  I  S  F  U  N  S
M  A  R  I  T  A  L  N  I
A  N  N  U  L  O  I  N  D
```

# CHAPTER 27 - FACTS AND IDEAS

**Directions:** Read the cases below and answer the questions that follow.

1. Immediately after Carl and Mindy's wedding reception, the two left for a honeymoon in France. On the second day of their honeymoon, Carl was struck by a bus and killed. Carl left no will. Does Mindy have any rights to Carl's separate property? Explain.

_____

_____

_____

_____

_____

_____

_____

_____

2. Jean and Larry cohabited together for fourteen years in Boulder, Colorado. Everyone in their community thought that they were legally married. Twelve years ago, they did have a wedding ceremony, but did not purchase a marriage license. Jean and Larry decided to move to Florida to start their own business. One day on her way to work, Jean was in a terrible accident and died. Does Larry have any rights to Jean's property?

_____

_____

_____

_____

_____

_____

_____

3. Sophie and Nicholas were in the process of dissolving their marriage. They have two children, Danny 8, and Victoria, 11. Both parents wanted custody of the children. In a heated custody case, the judge appointed Larry, an attorney, to represent the children. Is this legal? Explain.

_____

_____

_____

_____

_____

_____

_____

4. Maria, 38, has full custody of her 12-year old daughter, Daphne. When Maria lost her job she was unable to keep her home or to support Daphne. The state took Daphne away temporarily and put her in another family's home until Maria could get another job. Is this legal? Explain.

_____

_____

_____

_____

_____

_____

_____

# CHAPTER 27 - CRITICAL THINKING ACTIVITY

**Directions:** Write a Legal Focus Problem or a Legal Focus Example to demonstrate your understanding of the following concepts.

1. Community property _____

_____

_____

_____

_____

_____

_____

_____

_____

_____

2. Adoption _____

_____

_____

_____

_____

_____

_____

_____

_____

_____

_____

3. Prenuptial agreement _____

_____

_____

_____

_____

_____

_____

_____

_____

# CHAPTER 28 - VOCABULARY ACTIVITY

**Directions:** Fill in the blank with the correct term found in this chapter.

1. Property that is movable is called _____ property.

2. Land, buildings, and things permanently attached to the land is
   _____ property.

3. A temporary right to possess the personal property of another is a/n
   _____.

4. When there is only one owner to a piece of property it is called
   _____.

5. A type of co-ownership in which two or more persons share interests in a property;
   when one tenant dies the property interest passes to his or her heirs is known as a
   _____  _____  _____.

6. Personal property that has no physical existence is called _____
   property.

7. A co-ownership in which interest in the property passes to the surviving tenants if a joint
   owner dies is called _____  _____.

8. A co-ownership between husband and wife in which property interest transfers to the
   surviving spouse if one dies is _____  _____
   _____  _____.

9. A _____ is a voluntary transfer of property ownership
   without expecting anything in return.

10. Adding value to a piece of personal property by labor or materials is called
    _____.

11. Goods that are identical to every other item in its lot are called
    _____ goods.

12. A person giving a gift is called a/n _____.

13. Property that has been voluntarily placed somewhere by the owner and then forgotten
    is _____ property.

14. Property that the owner has voluntarily parted with, and has no intention of recovering
    is _____ property.

15. Property that the owner has involuntarily parted with, but cannot find is
    _____ property.

16. A person to whom possession of personal property is transferred is called the
    _____.

17. A bailment in which a bailee's duty of care is extraordinary is a
    _____ bailment.

# Chapter 28 - Facts and Ideas

**Directions:** Place an "R" in the blank if the property listed below is real property, place a "TP" in the blank if the property is tangible personal property, and an "IP" in the blank if the property is intangible personal property.

_____ 1. a computer

_____ 2. a garage unattached to a house

_____ 3. a patent to an invention

_____ 4. an automobile

_____ 5. copyrights on music

_____ 6. a speed boat

_____ 7. a $3,000 bond

_____ 8. an inground pool

Place a "B" in the blank if the story is an example of a bailment. Place a "G" in the blank if it is an example of a gift. Place an "S" in the blank if it is a sale.

_____ 9. Tracy rented an apartment for one year.

_____10. Don gave Michael his motorcycle in exchange for a stereo and $200.

_____11. Sally let Joan use her fur coat for a special occasion.

_____12. Denise promised to give Gary her record collection when he graduated from college.

_____13. Maury rented a car from Euro Rent for two weeks.

_____14. Sam brought his suit to a dry cleaners to be cleaned.

_____15. Troy gave his friend, Jim, his baseball card collection because Jim was moving away.

Place an "M" in the blank if the property being described is mislaid, an "L" in the blank if the property is lost, and an "A" if the property is abandoned.

_____ 16. Betty's checkbook fell out of her purse while in the grocery store. Betty went back the next day to look for it.

_____ 17. When Bruce got home, he noticed that he lost a $20 bill while in a restaurant. He decided not to worry about it.

_____ 18. Millie laid her purse on someone's car while she put her gloves on. She forgot about her purse and walked off. Fifteen minutes later she went back to look for her purse.

_____ 19. Danny accidentally dropped his camera while sightseeing in Rome.

_____ 20. Vivian left her coat on a chair in her neighbor's home. She decided to call her neighbor the next day to retrieve it.

# CHAPTER 28 - CRITICAL THINKING ACTIVITY

**Directions:** Read the story below containing references to property. Then decide which type of property ownership applies to each piece of property.

Jason buys a hotel with his friend, Gary, in Hyannis, Massachusetts. They both own and operate the hotel together. Jason and Gary have signed an agreement that states if one of them dies, the other will receive full interest of the hotel. Jason decides to marry Gwen. They reside in Boston, Massachusetts. During their marriage they bought a $250,000 home in Boston. Gwen inherited a cabin in Rockport, Massachusetts from her grandparents. She had been married to Jason for ten years when she received the cabin. Soon after receiving the cabin as an inheritance, Gwen decided to rewrite her will. Gwen included in her will that her sister is to receive Gwen's interest in the $250,000 home when she dies. Jason did not know about Gwen's desire to do this.

1. The hotel is a/n _____

   type of property ownership because _____

   _____

   _____

2. The $250,000 home is a/n _____

   type of property ownership because _____

   _____

   _____

3. The cabin is a/n _____

   type of property ownership because _____

   _____

   _____

4. Is Gwen's devise to her sister legal?  Why or why not? _____

_____

_____


5. What would the effects be on each of the transactions if Jason and Gwen lived in a community property state?

The hotel would _____

_____

The $250,000 home would _____

_____

The cabin would _____

_____

The devise to Gwen's sister would _____

_____


6. Does Jason have the right to transfer his ownership in the hotel to Gwen before he dies? Why or why not? _____

_____

_____

_____

# CHAPTER 29 - VOCABULARY ACTIVITY

**Directions:** Choose *ten* of the following vocabulary terms to define and give an example to demonstrate your understanding of the term.

adverse possession      conveyance
easement      eminent domain
escrow      fixture
license      profit
real estate closing      recording statute
quitclaim deed      warranty deed

1. Term: _____

   Definition: _____

   _____

   Example: _____

   _____

2. Term: _____

   Definition: _____

   _____

   Example: _____

   _____

3. Term: _____

   Definition: _____

   _____

   Example: _____

   _____

4. Term: _____

   Definition: _____

   _____

   Example: _____

   _____


5. Term: _____

   Definition: _____

   _____

   Example: _____

   _____


6. Term: _____

   Definition: _____

   _____

   Example: _____

   _____


7. Term: _____

   Definition: _____

   _____

   Example: _____

   _____

8. Term: _____

   Definition: _____

   _____

   Example: _____

   _____


9. Term: _____

   Definition: _____

   _____

   Example: _____

   _____


10. Term: _____

    Definition: _____

    _____

    Example: _____

    _____

# CHAPTER 29 - FACTS AND IDEAS

**Directions:** Answer the following questions with short statements.

1. Explain the importance between personal property and fixtures when buying or selling a home.

   _____

   _____

   _____

2. What is the major difference between a warranty deed and a quitclaim deed?

   _____

   _____

   _____

3. What risk do you take if you fail to record a deed?

   _____

   _____

   _____

4. What are the rights of the private property owner in eminent domain?

   _____

   _____

   _____

5. What is the difference between an easement and a profit?

_____

_____

_____

_____

6. What is the difference between an open listing and an exclusive listing?

_____

_____

_____

_____

7. Define nonpossessory interests and list the ones in this chapter.

_____

_____

_____

_____

8. What type of possession consists of obtaining title to the land without a voluntary transfer from the owner?

_____

_____

_____

_____

# CHAPTER 29 - CRITICAL THINKING ACTIVITY

**Directions:** Read the following story and answer the questions that follow.

Barbara and Thomas Lewis decided to sell their house and move to another city. Their home was custom built and contained handmade solid oak cabinets in the kitchen, custom draperies throughout the home, oriental throw rugs, marble sinks, and solid gold door knobs. The Lewis' lot is a beautifully 3-acre lot with the landscape including an herb garden, a flower garden, and three solid pine sitting benches. The Lewis' were asking $300,000 for their house. The Lewis' deed provided a clause that protects the buyer against any claims of ownership of the property by another party. The Lewis' grow evergreens on two acres of their property. They allow some of their neighbors to cut down their trees for the holiday season. After the Lewis' home was on the market for 60 days it was finally sold for $295,000. They set up an appointment with the broker to meet with the buyer to deliver the deed.

1. Which of the inside features of the Lewis' home are considered fixtures?

   _____

   _____

   _____

2. Which of the inside features of the Lewis' home are considered personal property?

   _____

   _____

   _____

3. Which of the outside features of the Lewis' home are considered real property or permanent fixtures?

   _____

   _____

   _____

4. Which of the outside features of the Lewis' home are considered personal property?

_____

_____

_____

5. What type of deed did the Lewis' offer?

_____

_____

_____

6. What type of right do the Lewis' give their neighbors when they allow them to take the evergreens?

_____

_____

_____

7. What is the appointment that the Lewis' made with the broker called?

_____

_____

_____

8. Could the Lewis' take the custom drapes and the solid gold door knobs with them when they move? Explain.

_____

_____

_____

# CHAPTER 30 - VOCABULARY ACTIVITY

**Directions:** Fill in the blanks with the proper term found in this chapter.

1. One to whom property is rented is called the _____.

   ____ ____ ____ ____ ____ ____

2. One who rents property to another is the _____.

   ____ ____ ____ ____ ____ ____ ____ ____

3. The process by which a landlord puts a tenant out of real property is called

   _____.

   ____ ____ ____ ____ ____ ____ ____ ____

4. When a landlord transfers the right to occupy land for a certain time in exchange for rent, it is a/n _____.

   ____ ____ ____ ____ ____

5. The landlord shall not disturb the tenant's use and enjoyment of the property during the lease term. This is referred to as the _____.

   ____ ____ ____ ____ ____ ____ ____ ____    ____ ____

   ____ ____ ____ ____ ____    ____ ____ ____ ____ ____ ____ ____ ____ ____

6. When a tenant destroys or abuses leased property without the landlord's consent, it is called _____.

   ____ ____ ____ ____ ____

7. When a landlord wrongfully performs or fails to perform an important promise required by the lease it is considered a/n _____.

___ ___ ___ ___ ___ ___ ___ ___ ___ ___ ___ ___

___ ___ ___ ___ ___ ___ ___ ___

8. The tenant's payment to the landlord for use of the real property is called _____.

___ ___ ___ ___

9. Money paid to the landlord to secure the tenant's obligations under the lease is called a/n _____.

___ ___ ___ ___ ___ ___ ___ ___    ___ ___ ___ ___ ___ ___ ___

10. Money a landlord charges a tenant for a late payment of the rent is a/n _____.

___ ___ ___ ___    ___ ___ ___ ___ ___ ___

11. When a landlord retakes possession of real property because of a breach by the tenant through a court procedure, it is called a/n _____.

___ ___ ___ ___ ___ ___ ___ ___

___ ___ ___ ___ ___ ___ ___ ___

12. A landlord's right to a tenant's personal property for failure to pay rent is a/n _____.

___ ___ ___ ___ ___ ___ ___ ___ ___    ___ ___ ___ ___

13. A _____ is when a tenant leases property to a third party.

   ____ ____ ____ ____ ____ ____ ____ ____


14. A tenancy for as long as both parties agree is called a/n _____.

   ____ ____ ____ ____ ____ ____ ____  ____ ____  ____ ____ ____ ____

# CHAPTER 30 - FACTS AND IDEAS

**Directions:** Read the scenarios below and answer the questions that follow.

1. Jane signed an agreement with Barry to lease his home for one year.

A. What term describes Jane's role in this transaction?

_____

B. What term describes Barry's role in this transaction?

_____

C. What type of lease has Jane signed?

_____


2. Bruce rents an apartment to Delores for $500 per month for as long as she needs the apartment. Delores agrees to pay Bruce $100 if her monthly payment is over five days late. Bruce also required Delores to pay $250 before signing the contract, in case something in the apartment is damaged.

A. What term describes the monthly $500 payment?

_____

B. What term describes the $100?

_____

C. What term describes the $250?

_____

D. What type of lease has Delores signed?

_____

3. Larry leases his home to Jeanette and her three children for one year. Jeanette has not paid her rent for three months. While Jeanette was not home, Larry entered her apartment and confiscated her television set as security.

A. Was Larry's act of taking Jeanette's television set legal? Explain.

_____

_____

_____

_____

B. What is the proper term for the right of a landlord to seize a tenant's personal property?

_____

C. What should Larry have done?

_____

4. Brett rents an apartment from Jack from month to month for $425 per month. The apartment has faulty electrical wiring and the outside is extremely unkempt. Brett decides to call the Occupational Safety and Health Association to motivate Jack to rectify some of these things. When Jack hears about Brett's complaints to OSHA, he evicts Brett.

A. What type of lease has Brett signed?

_____

B. What type of eviction has Jack filed? Explain.

_____

_____

_____

C. What can Brett do?

_____

_____

_____

# CHAPTER 30 - CRITICAL THINKING ACTIVITY

**Directions:** Read the cases below and advise the people on what they should do next. Write your answers in the blanks that follow the case. (Please be specific in your answers).

1. Serita rents an apartment from Jared for $675 per month. Serita has not paid her rent for four months. Jared has tried to contact Serita about the overdue rent, but she hangs up the telephone whenever he calls to speak with her.

   Jared should _____

   _____

   _____

   _____

   _____

   _____

   _____

2. Howard rents an apartment from Cathy for one year. Although the lease states nothing about subleasing, Howard allows Jennifer to rent his apartment when he takes a five month sabbatical. Cathy accepts the first check from Jennifer, but after the first rent payment, Jennifer never makes another payment.

   Cathy should _____

   _____

   _____

   _____

   _____

   _____

   _____

3. Create your own case by using an example about implied warranty of habitability on the following blanks.

_____

_____

_____

_____

_____

_____

_____

_____

_____

_____

_____

_____

_____

_____

_____

_____

_____

# CHAPTER 31 - VOCABULARY ACTIVITY

**Directions:** Fill in the blanks with the proper term found in this chapter.

1. An insurance contract is called a/n _____.

2. The person covered by an insurance contract is the _____.

3. The insurance company who sells the contract is the _____.

4. The money paid by the policyholder for insurance is the _____.

5. The prediction of a possible loss is called a/n _____.

6. When insurance companies spread the risk among many people it is called _____ _____.

7. A person must have a/n _____ _____, a real economic risk, in order to purchase insurance.

8. Ordinarily, the insured has a _____ _____, a fixed time after the due date, to pay the premium before the policy is canceled.

9. A type of life insurance that also provides a savings feature is called _____ _____.

10. _____ insurance covers accident, disability, and medical expense insurance.

11. The type of insurance that covers protection on a home and personal property is called _____ _____.

12. An insurance requiring the owner to insure his or her property up to a specified percentage of its value is called a/n _____ _____.

13. Automobile insurance that covers the insured for damages to his or her car resulting from a crash is called _____ insurance.

14. The insurance company's right to pursue any claims the policyholder would have against the wrongdoer is called _____.

15. The policyholder sometimes agrees to pay a _____, a certain amount of the loss of a claim.

16. Automobile insurance that pays beneficiaries if the policyholder dies in an automobile accident is called _____ _____ _____.

17. Automobile insurance that pays the insured for a hit-and-run driver is called

_____ _____

_____.

18. Automobile insurance that provides benefits to the insured, regardless of fault is called

_____ - _____

_____.

# CHAPTER 31 - VOCABULARY ACTIVITY

**Directions:** State the type of insurance that should be purchased for each of the following risks. All types of insurances used can be found in this chapter's textbook.

1. Sarah wants life insurance on her husband in case of his death. She wants the most inexpensive type.

   _____

2. Morris wants to purchase insurance in case he becomes unable to work because of an illness.

   _____

3. Samantha wants a policy to cover injuries incurred while on her property in case her friends or family are hurt.

   _____

4. Timothy wants coverage that will protect any harm to his automobile passengers if he is hit by someone who carries no automobile insurance.

   _____

5. Ronald wants to insure his personal possessions while leasing an apartment.

   _____

6. Millie wants her and her children's expenses covered in case of an illness.

   _____

7. Dillon wants to insure his car against theft.

   _____

8. Victoria wants to insure herself in the event that she is injured during an automobile accident.

   _____

9. Dr. Henry wants to purchase insurance in case he is sued because of a problem that could incur while treating a patient

_____

10. David wants to purchase an insurance that would cost him expenses in the event that the manager of his business dies.

_____

11. Deanna wants to purchase insurance that would cover hospital bills that could incur to passengers injured in an automobile accident while she is driving.

_____

12. Lyle wants insurance to cover damages for his car in case of an accident.

_____

Name_____ Date_____

# CHAPTER 31 - CRITICAL THINKING ACTIVITY

**Directions:** Read the case below and answer the questions that follow.

Mitch moved to a new city in California and decided that he needed more insurance coverage. He just built a new home and wanted to be sure that the house and the contents of the house are safe. Mitch is also concerned that his premium could possibly be a couple of days late some months because his pay check is mailed to him. Mitch would also like to purchase a life insurance policy for his wife. However, Mitch likes the idea of having a cash value to borrow from in case of an emergency. Finally, Mitch needs to add automobile insurance to his current automobile policy that would cover he and his wife and their automobile in the case of vandalism, since they have recently moved to a larger city.

1. What type of insurances should Mitch purchase for his home?

   _____

   _____

   _____

   _____


2. What type of life insurance should Mitch purchase?

   _____


3. What type of automobile insurance should Mitch purchase?

   _____

   _____

4. What advice would you give to Mitch on his purchase of :

A. homeowner's insurance?

_____

_____

_____

_____

B. life insurance?

_____

_____

_____

_____

C. automobile insurance?

_____

_____

_____

_____

# CHAPTER 32 - VOCABULARY ACTIVITY

**Directions.** Fill in the blanks with the appropriate term from this chapter. Then find and circle the term in the word search that follows.

1. A person's wishes for the distribution of his or her property after death is a/n _____.

2. When a person dies without leaving a will it is called _____.

3. A deceased person is referred to as a/n _____.

4. A gift of real estate by a will is a/n _____.

5. A gift of personal property by will is a/n _____.

6. A federal tax on property given to another after the death of the donor is a/n _____ tax.

7. The court responsible for administering any legal problems surrounding a will is a/n _____ court.

8. The person in charge of executing the will who is named in the will is a/n _____.

9. The person appointed by a court in charge of executing the will when one dies is the _____.

10. A properly documented written will is referred to as a/n _____ will.

11. A type of self-prepared will is a/n _____ will.

12. A written document that revokes or amends a will is a/n _____.

13. An arrangement in which property is transferred from one party to be administered by another to a third party beneficiary is a/n _____.

14. The person who holds property for another under a trust is called the _____.

15. A trust created during the grantor's lifetime is a/n _____ _____ trust.

16. A trust created in a will is a/n _____ trust.

```
L  A  D  M  I  N  I  S  T  R  A  T  O  R  T
W  O  A  R  N  E  L  O  W  O  R  C  H  A  T
M  I  L  O  T  E  L  A  G  R  A  P  O  L  S
Y  N  L  O  E  U  A  E  R  T  E  T  L  H  L
R  T  O  L  S  T  G  S  S  R  X  M  O  E  N
O  E  E  G  T  O  E  E  S  U  E  U  G  S  E
M  R  A  N  A  I  U  N  T  S  C  H  R  E  G
T  V  I  M  T  Q  L  D  R  T  U  W  A  O  N
C  I  L  D  E  C  E  D  E  N  T  O  P  A  M
H  V  I  B  T  H  L  E  S  I  O  S  H  H  I
F  O  C  N  E  A  E  V  T  B  R  S  I  A  S
U  L  I  N  M  I  P  I  A  I  G  E  C  T  S
A  L  D  R  H  O  E  S  T  R  U  S  T  E  E
P  R  O  B  A  T  E  E  E  T  M  O  R  E  A
O  F  C  T  E  S  T  A  M  E  N  T  A  R  Y
```

# CHAPTER 32 - FACTS AND IDEAS

**Directions:** Determine whether each of the following gifts are a devise or a bequest and whether it is a specific, general, or residuary gift.

1. You leave $10,000 from your savings account to your son.

   _____

2. You leave your 1963 Corvette to your uncle.

   _____

3. You leave your condominium in Orlando to your mother.

   _____

4. You leave your antique necklace to your daughter.

   _____

5. You leave the remainder of any monies to your spouse.

   _____

6. You leave whatever personal possessions that are left unnamed in your will you daughter.

   _____

Answer the following questions with short answers.

7. What are the requirements an individual must possess in order to make a legal will?

   _____

   _____

8. What is a nuncupative will?

_____

_____

9. What is the major objection to a holographic will?

_____

_____

10. If a child is not mentioned in the will, what will probably occur?

_____

_____

11. What are the responsibilities of a trustee?

_____

_____

12. What is the difference between an inter vivos trust and a testamentary trust?

_____

_____

# CHAPTER 32 - CRITICAL THINKING ACTIVITY

**Directions:** Read the case below and answer the questions that follow.

Richard decides to prepare a will. He contacts his lawyer, who sends Richard a pre-printed will with blanks to be completed by Richard. Richard decided to leave all of his real estate to his son, David; all of his jewelry to his daughter, Evelyn; and the remains of his personal property to his wife, Renee. Richard has a ten-year old grandson that he would like to leave a sum of money to. He appointed his lawyer, Samuel, to invest the money and distribute it to his grandson when he becomes 21 years old. This was written in the will.

1. What type of will did Richard prepare?

   _____

2. Who is the testator of the will?

   _____

3. What type of gift did Richard leave his son, David?

   _____

4. What type of gift did Richard leave his daughter, Evelyn?

   _____

5. What type of gift did Richard leave his wife?

   _____

6. What type of gift did Richard leave his grandson?

   _____

7. What role does the lawyer, Samuel, have in the grandson's gift?

   _____

8. What role does Richard's grandson have ?

   _____

9. Who is the settlor?

_____

10. What type of trust did Richard create?

_____


Create your own scenario and questions using other concepts from this chapter.

_____

_____

_____

_____

_____

_____

_____

_____

_____

_____

_____

_____

_____

_____

_____

_____

_____